Q20
H97

MW01001364

MINIATURE BOOKS

Their History

from the beginnings to the present day

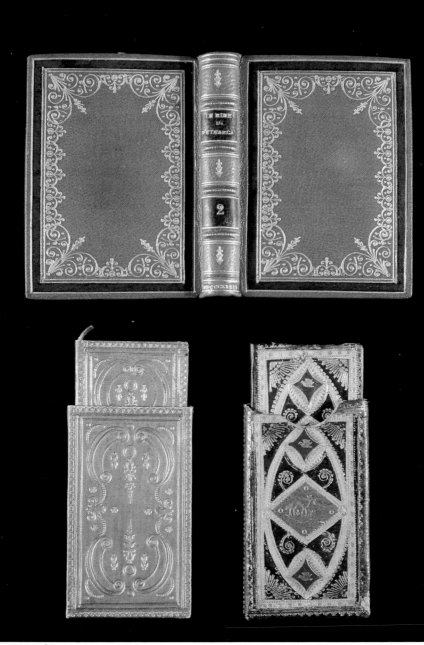

LE RIME DE PETRARCA,
Venice, Fred. Ongania, 1879.

THE LONDON
ALMANACK, 1855 and 1800
editions in slip cases.

MINIATURE BOOKS

BOOKS

THEIR HISTORY
from the beginnings
to the present day by

LOUIS W. BONDY

LONDON: SHEPPARD PRESS

First published: September 1981

I.S.B.N.: 0 900661 23 2

© Louis W. Bondy 1981

SHEPPARD PRESS LIMITED
Russell Chambers, Covent Garden
London W.C.2.

MADE IN ENGLAND
Printed for the publishers by NENE LITHO
and bound by WEATHERBY WOOLNOUGH.

FOREWORD

There may be other opinions, but most people with any knowledge of the subject would consider Louis Bondy to be the world's leading authority on miniature books. For nearly sixty years he has collected, bought, sold and studied these little miracles of the art of printing, as he calls them.

Born in Berlin in 1910, he is the son of a well-known journalist and, after studying architecture at the Technical University and in Geneva, he became a journalist himself, specialising in local affairs, book and theatre reviews.

In 1932 he went to Paris as correspondent of the **Deutsche Allgemeine Zeitung,** but was dismissed a year later when the National Socialists gained power in Germany. He went to Spain and, for a couple of years earned his living as a photographer, journalist and translator until, a few months after the outbreak of the Spanish Civil War, he came to England in 1936.

Eighteen months later he joined the Jewish Central Information Office (later the Wiener Library) where he was concerned with the historical and political evaluation of the Nazi press and literature. He became Acting Director of the Office and during the 1939–45 war was ranked as a temporary civil servant with the Political Intelligence Department of the British Foreign Office. After the war he attended the Nuremberg Trials of war criminals and his book **Racketeers of Hatred** was published.

All this time Louis Bondy had been gathering rare and interesting books, especially miniature volumes of which he had been an enthusiastic collector ever since he saw some in a bookshop as a child. In 1946 he opened his own antiquarian book shop in London and soon became known to dealers, collectors and librarians throughout the world. Since then he has issued more than ninety catalogues of fine and rare books for sale, nearly all of them containing a substantial number of valuable miniature items, and he has by lectures, articles and personal contact, communicated to countless others the fascination that these little treasures have for him.

ACKNOWLEDGE-
MENTS

Special thanks are due to Messrs. Christie's, the famous London auctioneers, for courteous permission to use photographs from their catalogues listing the Houghton Collection of Miniature Books, and I am particularly obliged to their Mr. Hans Fellner for his assistance in that respect.

I am also grateful to the British Library and its Staff for letting me inspect the contents of the miniature book cabinets at leisure and in detail.

My wife, Hannah, has greatly contributed to my understanding of the miniature book world by locating many items which were hitherto unknown to me. I would also like to thank Mrs. Christine Sutherland, my assistant and friend, for reminding me of many books worthy of mention, especially in the field of juvenilia.

A number of friends and clients abroad have earned my gratitude for bringing details of their collections, and public exhibitions of these treasures, to my notice. Miss Ruth E. Adomeit, Mr. Robert W. Bloch, Mr. Julian I. Edison and Mr. Stanley Marcus were most helpful in supplying such information.

Last but not least I would like to thank my publishers, and especially Mr. Trefor Rendall Davies, for the enthusiastic support given so cheerfully at all times in preparing this volume for the press.

L.W.B.

MINIATURE BOOKS

THEIR HISTORY
from the beginnings
to the present day

CHAPTER ONE

WHY MINIATURE
BOOKS?

Miniature Books: Just two words but they open up an entire world, the very existence of which is unknown to many, even amongst the inner circle of collectors. In this book we shall endeavour to explore this tiny universe, discover its many wonders, explain its beauty as well as its intricacies and, perhaps, gain new friends for a stimulating and enticing aspect of bibliophily.

We begin by attempting to define the term "miniature books". The first consideration must, of course, be size. While opinions on this vary, the vast majority of collectors have opted for volumes the height and width of which does not exceed three inches, that is 76 millimetres. Three inches is a magical figure beyond which many collectors will refuse to go when assembling a miniature book library. Generally speaking I agree with them: the hobby must be governed by the calibrated ruler if it is to mean anything. Such a measurement includes the size of the binding and only the extreme purists have attempted to define dimensions by page size, or even by that of the part of the page actually covered by print.

It is, however, my firm opinion that in a few

1

exceptional cases where very small print is combined with a characteristic and carefully conceived miniaturisation of binding and design, slightly larger volumes should be included in a miniature book collection. Some such volumes are described in the following chapters, chiefly those of travelling libraries and the famous Diamond Classics published by William Pickering in London.

Discerning minibibliophiles may on the other hand rule out some volumes measuring less than three inches when they are crudely and carelessly printed in large type, when their bindings are decorated in an uncharacteristically ill-proportioned way and where the use of thick and poorly constituted paper swells the books to lumpy and unattractive fatness.

Some collectors only wax enthusiastic when encountering very small volumes, perhaps under two inches or even under one inch high, while collectors of dolls' houses have to limit themselves to volumes which have the right proportions in relation to the small rooms and pieces of furniture.

In this book we shall try to describe a great variety of miniature books and thus cater for many different tastes and interests. Subjects will range from the literature of many lands and epochs to history, medicine and science, botany and fauna, religion and philosophy, topography and travel, gastronomy and philately, art and reference works. Even politics and erotica have not infrequently hidden their more secretive purposes in the pages of very small books. On the other hand it will surprise nobody to come across a large number of children's books, as the tiny format has always had a very special appeal for the young

We might ask ourselves, however: Why collect miniature books at all? What is so special about them? What makes enthusiasts eagerly scan catalogues, queue up at auction sales, wander from bookshop to bookshop, gaze at the displays of antique dealers, when quite often the same text can be bought in a larger volume at a tiny fraction of the price of a miniature edition?

For those of us who have been bitten by this particular bug, the answer is easy. The first advantage is extreme portability. The works of a beloved poet, the text of a play that we are going to see on stage, the classical texts important to scholars, the words of a foreign language and their equivalent in our own, scientific formulae or technological details needed for work or study, religious works like Bibles, prayer or hymn books to carry to church, can all be available when we need them. Without much difficulty we can, if we wish, keep a small library in our pockets or handbags. In addition, such a miniature library will take up very little space in our small modern houses and flats, and at the same time constitute a decorative and charming centre of attraction.

Equally important is the fact that the production of very small books has always taxed craftsmen to the extreme and compelled them to give of their very best under most difficult and challenging circumstances. Thus printers have created and used tiny type of great legibility and often of unparalleled beauty; binders have striven to match the delicate handling of the finest leathers with tooling and lettering designed to harmonise with the proportions appropriate to the small format; silver and gold smiths have surpassed themselves in producing stunningly beautiful filigree bindings and clasps; illustrators and engravers have had to learn the difficult art of giving expression to their talents and skills by creating pictures often covering less than a square inch. Even the manufacture of printing papers has been advanced beyond its ordinary limits by the need to make use of the thinnest possible paper in the production of multipaged volumes like minute, complete Bibles, dictionaries and encyclopedias, long plays and novels, which otherwise would have become too bulky.

The human race has always hankered after extremes. In the same way that it has tried to climb the highest mountains, explore the profoundest depths of the oceans, build the biggest and tallest buildings, it has always been enthralled by the smallest. Dwarfs and flea circuses, the amoebae visible only under a microscope, the Lord's Prayer written on a cherry stone, dolls' houses with their tiny furniture and crockery, Baxter's needle prints and miniature sculptures are witnesses to this interest in and love of the minute.

In this small world, books occupy a place of honour. They join to the great skill lavished on their creation the crowning glory of man's spirit enshrined in their text. Small wonder then that the ranks of collectors who specialise in them and who cherish, nay adore, them, is forever growing while more and more miniature books of high quality are being produced in many countries, assuring future generations of a continuing supply. An ever increasing number of people are convinced of the dictum that small is beautiful. We are thus setting out with confidence and enthusiasm on our journey through the history of these remarkable volumes.

SEPTEM PSALMI PENITENTIALES. An example of a 17th century miniature manuscript, almost indistinguishable from printing. Made at Antwerp for Francesco Baglier Patigino of Rome.

CHAPTER TWO

FROM THE BEGINNINGS TO THE END OF THE SIXTEENTH CENTURY

Miniature books preceded the invention of printing around the middle of the fifteenth century. The earliest example of such a "book" known to us is a Sumerian cuneiform clay tablet sold at auction in London as the oldest item in the remarkable collection of Arthur A. Houghton, Junior. It measures $1\frac{5}{16}$ by $1\frac{5}{8}$ inches and dates back to the years 2060 and 2058 before the birth of Christ and its text contains details of the issue of gold, precious stones and copper. The same sale included an Italian miniature manuscript of Virgil's **Aeneid** on a vellum scroll, $2\frac{5}{8}$ inches wide and over 100 inches long dating from the beginning of the 15th century. Many other early miniature manuscripts exist and during the second half of the 15th century a great number of beautiful small manuscripts were produced, often finely illuminated, of which quite a few have survived. They command now very high prices indeed.

Our chief concern lies, however, with the printed book. As may be imagined, very few true miniature incunabula, books printed before 1501, now exist. Nevertheless, the Library of Congress in Washington possess an **Officium Beatae Virginis Mariae,** printed by Mathias Moravius in Naples in 1486, measuring 3 by 2 inches in its binding. It also owns a **Tesauro Spirituale** by Bernardinus de Bustis, published in Lyons 1500-1501, measuring $2\frac{3}{16}$ by 2 inches. Another incunabulum of small dimensions, but slightly exceeding our 3-inch limit, is an **Alphabetum Divini Amoris,** attributed to Johannes Gerson, published in Basle by Johann of Amerbach ca. 1491. It is in the famous Newberry Library in Chicago and measures $3\frac{3}{8}$ by $2\frac{3}{8}$ inches. Kurt Freyer, in **Mikrobiblion,** mentions a tiny **Regula Sancti Benedicti,** printed around 1490 in Milan by Jacobus de Sancto Nazaro de la Ripa on parchment, the printed portion of which is about $2\frac{5}{8}$ inches high. A few other miniature incunabula have been mentioned, but no exact details are available.

The sixteenth century brings a much richer harvest. Pride of place must be given to two splendid Hours of the Virgin according to the use of Rome,

5

both printed on vellum. The first is **Officium Beate Marie Virginis secundum consuetudinem romane curie,** published by Lucantonio Giunta in Venice on May 4th, 1506, with six finely illuminated full-page woodcuts, measuring $2\frac{7}{8}$ by $2\frac{1}{16}$ inches. The second is **Hore Beate Marie Virginis secundum verum usum romanum,** printed in red and black with 14 full-page and 3 smaller fine illuminated woodcuts, published by Thielman Kerver in Paris in 1514, measuring $2\frac{9}{16}$ by $1\frac{5}{8}$ inches. It is exquisitely printed in italic type and struck me as one of the most beautiful and inspired pieces of miniature book production imaginable when I had the pleasure of handling it. At the Houghton sale in December 1979, the first book of hours fetched £3500, the second £10,000.

Another book of the highest quality, a copy of which was in my possession for many years, is the extremely rare **Kalendarium Gregorianum,** printed in red and black by the famous Christopher Plantin in Antwerp in 1585. It is by far the smallest book issued from that famous press and measures only $1\frac{3}{8}$ by $\frac{7}{8}$ inches. As far as we know, only two copies of this splendid volume have survived. The date of its publication follows by only three years the introduction of the Gregorian Calendar in 1582.

Very few genuine miniature books of the sixteenth century have successfully weathered the storms of that turbulent period. Most if not all of them are religious works. The **Psalterium Secundum Ordinem Bible,** published in Saragossa *in edibus Georgii Coci* in 1560, measures $2\frac{5}{8}$ by $1\frac{11}{16}$ inches. A small Dutch edition of the Psalms, translated from the French, was issued in Leiden by Jan Paedts Jacobszoon and Jan Bouwenszoon in 1590, being $2\frac{13}{16}$ inches high and $1\frac{13}{16}$ inches wide. **Septem Psalmi Poenitentiales** was printed by Guglielmo Faciotto in Rome in 1596, measuring $2\frac{5}{16}$ by $1\frac{7}{8}$ inches while **Mikrobiblion** lists a 1592 edition of the same book.

Two **Newe Testament** editions were published in London by the Deputies of Christopher Barker in 1593 and 1598, measuring $2\frac{15}{16}$ by 2 inches and $2\frac{7}{8}$

by 1$\frac{15}{16}$ inches respectively. They mark the beginnings of English miniature book production which was to take such a fascinating turn early in the next century, with the appearance of an extraordinary crop of much smaller volumes, which are now counted amongst the greatest treasures in the field; but in beauty of conception and details of design, in strength of character and supreme craftsmanship, the miniature Books of Hours of the beginning of the sixteenth century bear comparison with the finest productions of later years. While they lack perhaps the playful inventiveness that gradually crept into the manufacture of these miracles of printing which is reaching its pinnacle — or perhaps its extremity — only in the concluding years of this century, they bear in their tiny compass a witness to the strong religious feelings and convictions, and the artistic perfection which dominated the period.

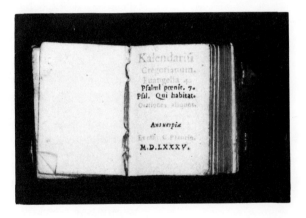

KALENDARIUM GREGORIANUM. Antwerp, C. Plantin, 1585.

CHAPTER THREE

THE SEVENTEENTH CENTURY,

A SWELLING TIDE

Great printers like Aldus, Giunta, Paganino, Plantin and others were among the first to introduce small books that may be termed pocket editions of the classics. Their's were the "Penguin Books" and "Reclam Editions" of the early years and more than a few of them have found their way into various miniature book collections and bibliographies. We must, however, reject them in this context because they are too large in size, and lack the extraordinary miniaturisation which must guide us in our selection. On the other hand, the very beginning of the new century brought a spate of true miniature classics, genuine and scholarly editions with carefully edited texts which were eminently pocketable and may have been carried by their owners when wandering through the cloisters of their monasteries or the quadrangles of their universities.

Outstanding examples are the Cicero, **De Officiis,** published in Antwerp by the Officina Plantiniana Raphelengii in 1606, printed in fine roman and italic type, measuring $2\frac{3}{16}$ by $1\frac{7}{8}$ inches, and Epictet's **Enchiridion** followed by the **Tabula** of Cebes, issued by the same press under the management of Plantin's son-in-law in 1616, measuring $2\frac{13}{16}$ by $1\frac{13}{16}$ inches.

Other beautiful editions of the Latin and Greek classics are due to Jean Jannon of Sedan whose famous Horace was published in 1627 which with a measurement of $3\frac{3}{16}$ by $1\frac{13}{16}$ inches slightly exceeds our limit, as does his Virgil, dated 1625 which measures $3\frac{1}{4}$ by $1\frac{1}{4}$ inches. Jannon also published a celebrated **Novum Testamentum Graecum** in 1628, measuring $3\frac{1}{4}$ by $1\frac{7}{8}$ inches, printed in a superb tiny Greek type, *la petite sédanoise,* which has been highly praised by many bibliographers and printing experts as the finest ever created for a miniature edition. The same printer also published a French edition of **Les Pseaumes de David,** *mis en rime françoise par Clément Marot et Theodore de Bèze,* dated 1626 and measuring $2\frac{9}{16}$ by $1\frac{13}{16}$ inches.

A lovely edition of the book **De Constantia** by the Belgian writer Justus Lipsius (1547-1606) was

8

published by Janssonius in Amsterdam in 1631. It has a fine engraved frontispiece showing a female figure holding a sword above a fire, and measures $2\frac{7}{8}$ by $1\frac{7}{8}$ inches. **De Consolatione Philosophiae,** a renowned work by the Roman philosopher and poet Boethius, made its appearance in several miniature editions. The earliest known to us is that published by Raphelengius in his Officina Plantiniana in Antwerp in 1610. It measures $2\frac{11}{16}$ by $1\frac{3}{4}$ inches. Another small edition of that beautiful and poetic text, much loved during the renaissance, is that issued by G. J. Caesius in Amsterdam in 1625, measuring $2\frac{5}{8}$ by $1\frac{11}{16}$ inches. It has a fine engraved title. Two further editions of Boethius were issued in Leyden by J. Maire in 1620, edited by Petrus Bertius and measuring $2\frac{13}{16}$ by $1\frac{3}{8}$ inches, and by the Officina Baltazaris Belleri in Douai in 1632, $2\frac{15}{16}$ by $1\frac{7}{8}$ inches.

De Imitatione Christi, by Thomas à Kempis, perhaps next to the Bible the most widely reprinted religious work, exists in many miniature editions right up to the present day. Mention should be made of two seventeenth century ones; that published by Cornelius ab Egmond in Cologne in 1629 edited by the Jesuit H. Rosweidus and printed in a very clear, tiny type, with engraved title and one plate, size $2\frac{3}{4}$ by $1\frac{1}{4}$ inches, and the edition of the Plantin Press of Balthasar Moretus in Antwerp, 1652, measuring 3 by 2 inches.

The British Library has on its shelves a very rare edition of the **Aphorisms of Hippocrates, ex interpretatione Joannes Heurnii,** published in Ingolstadt *ex typis Ostermayrianis* in 1680, measuring $2\frac{7}{8}$ by $1\frac{15}{16}$ inches. It has 173 numbered and 17 unnumbered pages. The rare first edition of **Horologium Auxiliaris Tutelaris** by the German Jesuit mystic Hieremias Drexelius or Drechsel appeared in Douai *ex Typographia Baltazaris Belleri* in 1623, measuring 3 by 2 inches. It is not often that we see a significant book published in its original edition in the miniature format.

The Psalms of David are found in many editions and in different languages. Dr. Percy Spielmann lists some in the catalogue of his library under nos. 423 to 428, but all of them exceed our 3-inch limit. In the Houghton sale there was the only known copy of **The Whole Book of Psalmes collected into English Meeter** by Thomas Sternhold, John Hopkins and others, London, for the Company of Stationers, 1606, measuring $2\frac{13}{16}$ by $1\frac{13}{16}$ inches. Like many 17th century editions that volume is in a fine embroidered needlework binding. An Italian edition of the seven penitential psalms and many prayers, **Li Sette Salmi Penitentiali et Molte Divote Orationi** appeared in Venice, Misserini, in 1628. Printed in red and black, its size is $2\frac{1}{8}$ by $1\frac{3}{8}$ inches. Three other editions of the psalms merit special attention. The one is the Swedish **Een Lillen Psalm-Bok,** published by Zacharias Brockenius in Strengnas in 1661, $2\frac{1}{2}$ by $1\frac{7}{16}$ inches, the earliest Swedish miniature book known to us. The others are two editions in the German translation by Ambrosius Lobwasser with music, the one published by Andreas Schimmel in Danzig in 1648, measuring $2\frac{7}{8}$ by $1\frac{3}{4}$ inches, the other the **Psalmen Davids Ambrosii Lobwassers, sampt andern Geistlichen Liedern, Psalmen und Kirchengebetten,** issued by Johann Ammon in Frankfurt in 1627, $2\frac{7}{16}$ by $1\frac{1}{2}$ inches. I have seen both these volumes clothed in outstanding bindings, the first in calf with fine brass clasps, the second in a very handsome embroidered binding decorated with pearls and sequins. Such bindings bear witness to the high esteem in which miniature books were held, even at such an early date.

The British Library possesses a rare devotional book in German, entitled **Christlich Gesang-Büchlein** followed by a second part **Andächtiges Betbüchlein,** edited by Johann Jepp. This little Christian Song Book, followed by the Devotional Prayer Book was published at Ulm in 1648 and printed by Balthasar Kühne. It has an engraved frontispiece and title of exceptional quality and measures $1\frac{7}{8}$ by $1\frac{3}{8}$ inches.

Several very small books of considerable importance from both a literary and sociological point of view were published in London during the early years of the seventeenth century. Amongst these, **The Tale of Troy** by the Elizabethan playwright and poet, George Peele, ranks very highly. It was issued by Arnold Hatfield in 1604 and is the first edition in book form. The only known surviving copy, measuring $1\frac{1}{4}$ by 1 inches, was auctioned by Christie's in their prodigious sale of the Houghton collection on the 11th June, 1980.

Martin Parker's **An Abstract of the Historie of the Renouned Maiden Queene Elizabeth** is also known in only one copy which passed from the Chatsworth Collection of the Duke of Devonshire

AN ABSTRACT OF THE HISTORIE OF THE RENOUNED MAIDEN QUEENE ELIZABETH.
London, Thomas Cotes, 1631. Title-page.

11

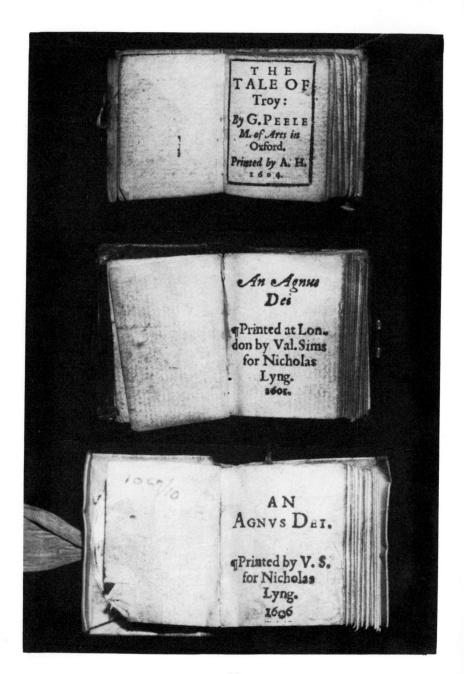

THE
TALE OF
Troy:
By G. PEELE
M. of Arts in
Oxford.
Printed by A. H.
1 6 0 4.

An Agnus
Dei

¶Printed at Lon-
don by Val. Sims
for Nicholas
Lyng.
1605.

AN
AGNVS DEI.

¶Printed by V. S.
for Nicholas
Lyng.
1606

into the hands of Arthur A. Houghton and was sold on the same day as the **Tale of Troy.** It relates briefly "the principall matters throughout her long and glorious raigne in English meeters" and was published by Thomas Cote in 1631, measuring $2\frac{1}{2}$ by $1\frac{1}{2}$ inches. It is listed in S.T.C. under No. 19217.5. Parker, who died around 1656, was commended by Dryden as the best ballad-writer of his day, the very ephemeral nature of this unique surviving copy thus lending this miniature volume even greater significance.

Almost equally rare are two editions of John Weever's **An Agnus Dei,** a life of Christ in verse, published in London and printed by V. Sims for N. Lyng. The first is dated 1601 and measures $1\frac{7}{16}$ by $1\frac{1}{16}$ inches, the other copy being the third edition, dated 1606 and measuring $1\frac{7}{16}$ by $1\frac{3}{16}$ inches. Both were sold at the recent Houghton sale and only one other copy of each is known to exist. Altogether, the Short Title Catalogue of English Books (Second edition) lists four different miniature editions of this title, three of them as being in the libraries of notable miniature book collectors, Julian I. Edison, Arthur Houghton and Julia P. Wightman. The dates are 1601, 1603, 1606 and 1610, and their format is described as "128o?".

We were fortunate to find another very rare early English miniature book of which, as far as we know, only one copy has survived. It is **The Booke of Martyrs** by John Taylor, called the Water Poet and has two parts. It was printed in London for John Hamman in 1616 and measures $1\frac{11}{16}$ by $1\frac{3}{8}$ inches. The first part has a curious dedicatory poem to William Earle of Pembrooke which reads: "My Lord, my weake collection out hath tooke The sum and pith of the great Martyrs Booke. For Pardon and Protection I entreate, The volums little, my presumption great". Listed in my catalogue 64/1964 under no. 435 and in S.T.C. under no. 23731.3, that copy is now in the Bodleian Library. Later miniature editions are dated 1617, 1627, 1631 and 1633.

Together with the **Verbum Sempiternum** and

VERBUM SEMPITERNUM,
by John Taylor. Two rare
editions, Aberdeen, 1670 and
London, 1693.

Salvator Mundi by the same John Taylor (1580-1653), Weever's **An Agnus Dei** started the fashion of the so-called thumb Bibles, tiny abbreviated histories of the Bible in prose or verse, chiefly intended for children. They flourished mightily during the 18th and 19th centuries and a later chapter is devoted specially to them.

John Taylor's above-mentioned two titles (in one volume) were first published in London in 1614 and printed for J. Hamman by J. Beale. S.T.C. lists only one copy of that edition, in the possession of Ruth E. Adomeit, an American miniature book collector and bibliographer of note. The size is simply described as 64mo. Other early editions include the very rare one published by John Forbes in Aberdeen, 1670 (see illustration), measuring $1\frac{11}{16}$ by $1\frac{7}{16}$ inches, of which Houghton possessed one of the only two copies listed by Wing. Present-day collectors who are setting out in pursuit of copies of this pleasantly rhymed little volume, will have a better chance of finding copies if they search for one of the two 1693 editions. The first is that printed by F. Collins in London for T. Ilive, size $1\frac{7}{8}$ by $1\frac{7}{16}$ inches, the second edition, "with amendments", of the same size, bears only the T. Ilive imprint. Wing lists these editions under Nos. T 525 and 526. Many more editions followed during the next century and the latest, reprinting the 1693 edition, were published by Longman in London around 1850, clothed in renaissance bindings with metal clasps. The great popularity of these texts is perhaps explained by the fact that this Thames waterman turned poet had, as Harvey's **Oxford Companion to English Literature** remarks, "a marked talent for expressing himself in rolicking verse and prose".

While neither Weever nor Taylor specifically describe their works as children's books, we find in our records at least two 17th century miniature books expressly written for young people. The first is **Gantz neues Kinder ABC. Das Biblische Spruch- und Guldne Abc, teutsch und lateinisch, für die Jugend in diese kleine Form**

gebracht, (An entirely new Children's ABC, the Biblical and Golden ABC in German and Latin, presented in this small format for young people). It was published during the 17th century without place name or date by J. A. Hillemann and measures only $\frac{3}{16}$ by $\frac{3}{16}$ inches. Gumuchian, No. 13 lists the tiny volume as of the greatest rarity. The second title is **Kern der Godlyke Wahrheden voor de Jeugd,** (Kernel of Godly Truths for Young People) published in Amsterdam in 1700, with engraved title and 8 plates, 124 pages, size 2 by $1\frac{3}{8}$ inches. It is listed under no. 77 in the list of miniature books in the Grolier Club, New York.

An enchanting pictorial Bible entitled **Des Alten (Des Neuen) Testaments Mittler** is not specifically intended for children. The 263 finely executed small plates, imaginatively and beautifully engraved by the sisters Christina and Magdalena Küslin, or Küsel, are a pleasure to peruse and the calligraphic German text explains briefly and clearly the Bible passages illustrated by this 'Communicator' of the Old and New Testaments. The size of the book is $2\frac{1}{8}$ by $1\frac{11}{16}$ inches and it is undated. The two sisters were members of a brilliantly talented family of Augsburg engravers. Their father Melchior married a daughter of the great Matthias Merian whose grand-daughters they thus were. We can assume that these volumes were published in Augsburg and they certainly appeared towards the end of the 17th century (see Thieme-Becker, vol. 22, 74). Christie's catalogue of the Houghton miniature book sale, no. 277, speculates (with a question mark) that the volumes were published in Switzerland. Singer, **Allgemeines Künstler-Lexikon,** page 405, mentions this edition as does Tissandier, **Livres Minuscules,** page 6. These titles are very rare, and most desirable additions to any collection.

A similar pictorial Bible, which however slightly exceeds our 3-inch limit, is **Biblia Ectypa Minora Veteris Testamenti Historias Sacras et Res Maximi Momento Exhibentia, aeri incisa,** followed by the **Novum divini Nostri Iesu**

Christi Testamentum. Published by Christoph Weigel in Augsburg in 1696, it measures $3\frac{3}{8}$ by $2\frac{1}{8}$ inches, but the portion of the page covered by the engravings is only $2\frac{5}{8}$ inches high. I once possessed a copy and can say without a doubt that the 152 engraved plates which are certainly due to Weigel's hands, must rank amongst the finest illustrations ever produced in miniature form. According to the title, the book was specifically intended for young people.

As we have seen, the seventeenth century is rich in important and often beautiful miniature books. To these must be added some others which attract interest chiefly because of their curious and unusual nature.

Amongst the most extraordinary volumes are the all-engraved editions of the **Whole Book of Psalms in Meter** and the **New Testament** in the

DIE HEILIGE SCHRIFT ALT UND NEUEN TESTAMENTS. Nürnberg, Christoph Weigel, ca. 1700. Illustrations to books of the prophets.

shorthand of Jeremiah Rich, a leading stenography specialist of the period (circa 1660) who perfected the system invented by his uncle, William Cartwright, but without giving him credit, claiming it to be his own invention. The late Percy E. Spielmann had copies of the New Testament and of the Psalms in his collection. The Testament was printed for Wm. Marshall at ye Bible in Newgate Street & G. Marshall at ye Bible in Gracechurch Street and was described as the twentieth edition; almost certainly, these editions were very small, perhaps not comprising more than twenty copies each, judging by the rarity of these volumes. When cataloguing the Spielmann collection, it was dated as circa 1665. It bears a portrait of Rich, engraved by Thomas Cross and has an engraved title spelt out in shorthand only. It measures $2\frac{11}{16}$ by $1\frac{3}{4}$ inches. At the end there are two leaves, giving in attractive calligraphy "the Names of the Subscribers to this Incomparable Worke", just over forty names, including a Mr. Swintin, Secritary to ye Earle of Manchester, Thomas Lascells and the Lady Backhouse. Some late subscribers had their names squeezed in in tiny lettering.

The Spielmann copy of the Psalms, "according

DAS ALTEN TESTAMENTS MITTLER, late 17th Century. Three of the fine plates engraved by the sisters Küslin.

18

to the Art of Short-Writing written by Jeremiah Rich Author and Teacher of the said Art", was printed for the Author and "to be sould at his house the Golden Ball in Swithins Lane neare London Stone". It measures $2\frac{3}{8}$ by $1\frac{9}{16}$ inches, also has a frontispiece with Rich's portrait and at the end a short list of "the Names of those Ingenious Persons of my Schollars that were the first Incouragers of this incomparable peice". Other editions, all published around the year 1660, were "sold by Samuel Botley over against Vintners Hall" or "at Colonel Masons Coffee House in Cornhill", or published "for the author and sold by Henry Eversden". All the copies we have seen are extremely well engraved, showing hardly any signs of wear and must have taken years to produce. Their manufacture did evidently require a very steady hand and infinite patience. Most copies are beautifully bound in contemporary black morocco and are finely gilt-tooled. They were obviously

THE PSALMS IN SHORTHAND, by Jeremiah Rich. London, Samuel Botley, ca. 1660.

prized possessions and have remained most desirable collector's items to this date, notwithstanding the fact that hardly anyone will nowadays be able to decipher their obsolete shorthand.

Of even greater curiosity value, perhaps, is a volume the size of a finger-nail which was printed by Smidt in 1674, probably in Amsterdam, a town to which Benedikt Smidt had moved from Middelburg in 1673. It is the **Bloem-Hofje** by C. van Lange which for over 200 years was to remain the smallest printed book in existence. This fairly unimportant short Dutch poem must have been printed in such microscopic format in order to create a sensation and boost the art of the young printer who had so recently moved to the big city. Horodisch, in an article, *Uber Bücher kleinsten Formats* mentions that the production of such a tiny volume was only made possible through a trick. The text was printed in double spreads on one side of the paper only and then stuck together. Nevertheless, the end product is staggering and its significance, at least in the eyes of the printer, is underlined by the fact that the few known copies are all magnificently bound in gilt-tooled red leather with a finely chased gold clasp. They must have made stunning presents perhaps for a lady love, and have undoubtedly helped to awaken a passion for miniature books in many future collectors.

This chapter on the 17th century cannot be concluded without mentioning that according to Doris Welsh, a former librarian at the Newberry Library in Chicago and a great expert on miniature books, the first American miniature volume was William Secker's **A Wedding Ring fit for the Finger,** published in Boston by Samuel Green for T. Harris in the year 1690, measuring $2\frac{7}{8}$ by $1\frac{7}{8}$ inches.

BLOEM-HOFJE. Holland, 1673. For over two hundred years this was considered to be the smallest printed book.

CHAPTER FOUR

THE EIGHTEENTH CENTURY — AN EVER-GROWING LOVE OF SMALL BOOKS

We are now moving into an era well-known for its sophistication, refinement and grace. Small wonder that miniature books should follow this general trend. Beautiful little objects fitted more closely into this new and elegant world. Women and children were now admitted much more freely to the hitherto mainly masculine domain of books, and tiny books in particular were much more frequently specially designed for them. In the wake of such developments they became more wordly and less austere. Although thumb Bibles and similar religious volumes flourished and service and prayer books continued to have a large share in the production of miniature books right up to the early years of the twentieth century, we now witness the appearance of the first non-religious children's books and the beginning of an ever-increasing flood of often spirited and amorous almanacs.

The most remarkable tiny books of the century were perhaps the children's books published by Thomas Boreman in London in the early 1740's. These **Gigantick Histories** were thus entitled by their publisher because Boreman's bookshop was situated "near the two Giants in Guildhall", the famous Gog and Magog. These far from gigantic books were between $2\frac{3}{8}$ and $2\frac{1}{2}$ inches high and $1\frac{7}{8}$ inches wide. They were bound in flowered Dutch boards, attractively patterned. With their lists of child subscribers and attractive woodcut illustrations, simple texts and interesting London subjects, they must have made ideal presents for young people, fashioned as they were more for pleasure and entertainment than for moral improvement or instruction. It is generally assumed that Boreman was not only the publisher but also the author of these charming volumes which have of late not only become excessively rare but also very expensive. The titles are: **The Gigantick History of the two famous Giants and other Curiosities in Guildhall, London,** followed by **Volume the Second: Which completes the History of Guildhall, London. With other curious Matters.** They are dated 1740 and have 112 and 128 pages. The list of subscribers includes masters Neddy and Tommy Boreman, presumably the author's children, and the first volume is dedicated "to all the little masters and all the little misses who are in London town". A more official dedication is addressed to "their Royal Highnesses Prince George-William-Frederick, Duke of Cornwal, Prince Edward-Augustus and Princess Augusta" by "their affectionate servant". In 1741, there appeared **Curiosities in the Tower of London,** two volumes, second edition, also **The History and Description of the famous Cathedral of St. Paul's,** in two volumes with the second one bearing the additional title "An Account of the Monument & the Fire of London" (see illustration); **Westminster Abbey ... by the Author of the Gigantick Histories** came out in 1742-3 and ran to three volumes. The final volume in this 10-volume series is **The History of Cajanus, the Swedish Giant. From his Birth to the Present Time. By the Author of the Gigantick Histories.** It is dated 1742.

THE HISTORY ... OF ST. PAUL'S, LONDON. One of the "Gigantick Histories" published by Thomas Boreman, London, 1741.

Some of the Boreman volumes bear special admonishments to the young readers to buy further volumes in the series. Just about fifty years later publishers of children's books discovered an easier way to ensure customers for their entire series; they created special bookcases holding the complete collection.

John Newbery, a pioneering publisher and author of children's books, produced at least one miniature book. Entitled **Nurse True Love's New Year Gift,** it came out in London ca. 1765, has 58 pages with many woodcuts and measures 3 by 2½ inches. The text includes a very early version of "The House that Jack Built".

Special mention must be made of the fine editions of the Greek classics by the Foulis press in Glasgow. They slightly exceed the 3-inch size but are clearly characterised by the miniaturisation of the type and frequently by the finely balanced decoration of their bindings. The title most frequently found is the **Pindar, ex editione**

PINDAR. Glasgow, R. & A. Foulis, 1754. In Greek.

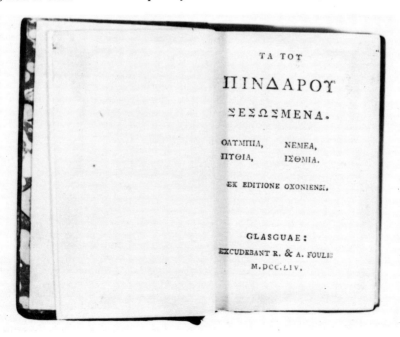

23

Oxoniensi. Printed by R. and A. Foulis in Glasgow, the volumes are variously dated from 1754 to 1759 and the complete set contains the Olympia, Pythia, Nemea and Isthmia. The size is $3\frac{1}{8}$ by 2 inches. A very few copies of the Olympia were printed on silk and are usually bound in attractively tooled red morocco. This makes them very precious and exceedingly rare miniature books, highly desirable but they are thicker than the copies printed on paper and the sober beauty of the fine Greek type is by no means enhanced. **Anacreon's Odes, with Sappho and Alcaeus,** 1751, $2\frac{7}{8}$ by $1\frac{7}{8}$ inches, is the other Foulis title said to exist printed on silk. The same Glasgow press also issued an Epictetus, **To tou Epiktetou Enchiridion,** edited by John Upton and published in 1751 and 1765. The size hovers around the $2\frac{15}{16}$ by $1\frac{7}{8}$ mark. Boswell bestowed high praise on the Foulis brothers by calling them "the Elzeviers of Glasgow".

Other remarkable 18th century miniature editions of the classics include the delightful Cicero **De Amicitia dialogus ad T. P. Atticum,** edited by J. G. Graevius, published by A. V. Coustelier in Paris in 1749 and a year later by C. J. B. Bauche in the same city, measuring $3\frac{1}{8}$ by $2\frac{1}{8}$ inches, with the printed portion of the page being less than 2 inches high. The edition is outstanding not only because of the finely cut type but also because of the engraved frontispiece signed by J. Robert and the attractive engraved title both printed in sanguine.

To these editions must be added one of the same title, printed in 1771 by Joseph Barbou in Paris, also with engraved portrait, measuring $3\frac{1}{2}$ by $2\frac{5}{16}$ inches, and Cicero's **Cato Major,** with a fine portrait by Ficquet after Rubens. Barbou printed that edition in 1758 with the very beautiful diamond $4\frac{1}{2}$-point type cut by P. S. Fournier, Jr., a fact specially mentioned on the last page. With $3\frac{7}{16}$ by $2\frac{5}{16}$ inches this title again exceeds our maximum size; but no rule can be without exceptions and we must strongly advise collectors to include this volume if they are lucky enough to find it.

Some outstanding 18th century miniature volumes

24

deal with historical subjects. **Kern der Nederlandsche Historie,** (The Essence of Netherlands History) consists of two parts in one very small tome, brilliantly illustrated with an engraved title and 36 finely executed plates. It was published in 1753 by T. Crajenschot in Amsterdam and has 266 pages. The size is $1\frac{11}{16}$ by $1\frac{1}{8}$ inches. Like the following item, it was intended for children and is now of considerable rarity. The **Kern der Kerkelyke Historie,** (The Essence of Church History) in two volumes was published by A. Blusse in Dordrecht in 1755 and also has 36 delightful engraved plates, including the title and a large folding plate. It is specifically dedicated to Dutch youth, measures $1\frac{13}{16}$ by $1\frac{1}{4}$ inches and has 556 pages. Not infrequently, only one of the two volumes turns up in shops or auctions. Collectors need not despair, however, of completing their set; I had for many years only the second volume in my collection, beautifully bound in contemporary red silk with silver clasp, which I had found in an Oxford bookshop. Nearly ten years later, I came across the first volume in identical binding while bookhunting in Brussels.

A miniature book of historical significance and great rarity is **La Constitution Française, décretée par l'Assemblé-Nationale Constituante aux années 1789, 1790 et 1791.** This important document of the French Revolution was printed in Paris in 1792 by the Imprimerie de la Société Litteraire-Typographique and measures $2\frac{5}{16}$ by $1\frac{13}{16}$ inches.

The smallest of all the 18th century books known to us, **'t Oranje Geslagt,** also deals with history. It was published in Groningen by H. Spoormaker in 1749 and measures only $\frac{5}{8}$ by $\frac{7}{16}$ of an inch. It contains doggerel rhymes on the kings of the family of Orange. It was produced in the same way as that described in the paragraph dealing with the 17th century Bloem-Hofje. Although copies are now very rare and the volume in the Houghton collection fetched £1100 in December, 1979, I remember being offered a number of these tiny treasures by a renowned Dutch bookseller some twenty-five years

't ORANJE GESLAGT.
Groningen, H. Spoormaker,
1749.

ago. According to the *Miniature Book Collector*, June 1960, an antique dealer in the Netherlands found a considerable number of copies of this hitherto unknown miniature book in a tortoise shell box he had acquired, where they had presumably been concealed ever since the days of their publication.

Another very small book of even greater rarity was listed in my Catalogue 67, no. 588, published in 1965. Its title is **La Joye sur le Retour de la Paix,** published in 1763 without indication of a place name. It measures 1 by $\frac{3}{4}$ inches and has 32 leaves. This copy was bound in light-blue velvet, decorated with gold thread. The book is dedicated to the King and the first page simply contains the words *Vive le Roi,* followed by a poem in praise of the sovereign and a love poem about shepherds and shepherdesses. We can find no reference to this elusive book.

Two collections of minute portraits of popular authors of the period were published in Germany around the year 1765 under the titles **Andenken der Gelehrten für das schöne Geschlecht,** (Souvenir of the Scholars, destined for the Fair Sex) and **Neujahrsgeschenk für das schöne Geschlecht** (New Year's Present for the Fair Sex). These two volumes measure ca. $\frac{7}{8}$ by $\frac{13}{16}$ of an inch and contain tiny engraved portraits of poets like Hagedorn, Klopstock, Haller and Lessing with amusing verse extolling their talents (see **Mikrobiblion,** No. 5 and Christie's catalogue of the Houghton sale, No. 248).

One of the rarest books in typographical literature also happens to be a miniature book. It is **A Short Account of the Rise and Progress of Printing, with a Compleat List of the First Books that were Printed.** Published by T. Parker in London ca. 1763, it has 123 pages and measures $2\frac{5}{16}$ by $1\frac{7}{16}$ inches.

Even sport found its way into 18th century miniature volumes. Gervase Markham's **The Young Sportsman's Instructor** exists in an early undated edition, London, ca. 1706, sold at the Gold

NEUJAHRSGESCHENK FÜR DAS SCHÖNE GESCHLECHT. 1765.

Ring in Little Britain. It is 2⅜ inches high, and is more common, although still very rare, in the reprint by J. Johnson of the Apollo Press for T. Gosden, London, 1820, measuring 2½ by 1¹¹⁄₁₆ inches. The book deals with "angling, fowling, hawking, hunting, ordering singing birds, hawks, poultry, coneys, hares and dogs, and how to cure them". I have seen a few copies both of the 18th century edition and of the reprint, the latter usually found in a very attractive binding with the design of a hunting horn stamped in gilt on both covers. Percy Spielmann's copy came from the splendid angling library of J. C. Lynn.

As befits the 18th century, the pleasures of love and lovemaking have been the subject of some miniature books. Of special interest is **De Flagrorum usu in re veneria. Et lumborum**

LE JOYEUX BOUTE-EN-TRAIN, "Paris, chez les amis de Piron", but in fact: Lille, chez Blocquel, ca. 1810.

27

renumque officio ... **libellus,** written by Johann Heinrich Meibom (Meibomius) who died in 1655. The edition is dated "London, 1665" but Brunet I, 677, states it to have been published in Paris in 1757. Such curious games of concealment were often played with books which have a certain "under the counter" nature and it is significant that neither publisher nor printer are mentioned. The volume has 79 pages and measures 3 by 2 inches. The learned German physician deals with the use of flagellation in medicine and sexual intercourse. The first edition was published in Leyden in 1639.

The seventeen-hundreds also saw the emergence of a number of very light-hearted song and poetry books. In the Netherlands, one title proved very popular and appeared in quite a number of small editions. It is **t'Groot Hoorns, Enkhuyser en Alkmaerder Liede-Boek, versiert meet veel mooye Bruylofts-liedekens en Gesangen** (A Song Book for the towns of Hoorn, Enkhuysen and Alkmaar, containing many beautiful wedding songs). One of the few dated editions we have seen is that published in Amsterdam by Pieter van Ryschooten in 1702, mesuring 3 by 2 inches. It has an amusing woodcut showing a room with a huge

THE YOUNG SPORTSMAN'S INSTRUCTOR ... by Gervase Markham. London, ca. 1708.

bed and the bride waiting for her newly-wed husband. Another more frequently found edition with the shorter title **t'Nieuw Groot Hoorns Lied-Boekje** was printed in Hoorn by Reinier Beukelman around 1750 and has the same size. Yet another edition, **t'Groot Hoorns, Enkhuyzer, Alkmaarder en Purmerender Liede-Boek,** Amsterdam, Johannes Kannewet, no date, measures $2\frac{7}{8}$ by $2\frac{1}{8}$ inches. The Houghton collection contained an earlier edition, published by Abraham van de Beeck in Hoorn in 1676, measuring $2\frac{13}{16}$ by $1\frac{13}{16}$ inches. All these editions contain wedding songs, many with music, and their text is frequently very outspoken and free although never lacking charm. They are often found in attractive contemporary bindings of morocco or shark-skin, with decorative silver clasps.

Around the year 1800, some frankly erotic little song books were published in Paris, amongst them **Chansons joyeuses de Piron, Collé, Gallet, etc.,** Saintin & Ledentu, measuring $2\frac{3}{8}$ by $1\frac{3}{4}$ inches. Two similar volumes of amorous poems and songs are **Chansonnier des Jours Gras, ou choix de chansons connues, érotiques, bacchiques, comiques...,** published by Antoine Beraud towards the end of the century, also measuring $2\frac{3}{8}$ by $1\frac{3}{4}$ inches, and **Les Jolies Gaillardises, ou le Chanteur en Goguettes,** with the amusing sentence added to the title in small print: "Aimables Demoiselles, pour que je chante il faut vous retirer", (Amiable ladies, you must retire before I can start singing). That volume, published anonymously in Paris under the fictitious imprint "Chez les Amis de la Joie", has 228 pages and measures $2\frac{3}{8}$ by $2\frac{1}{16}$ inches (see illustration). The two woodcut plates are very amusing but extremely naughty and allusive as far as their captions are concerned.

To return to the more traditional subject of theology, the 18th century provides some outstanding miniature examples. A book of hours, **Heures à la Cavalière,** was published by T. de Hansy in Paris in 1742 and again in 1751,

29

measuring $1\frac{15}{16}$ by $1\frac{3}{8}$ and $1\frac{5}{8}$ by $1\frac{1}{8}$ inches respectively. Various miniature **Heures de Cour,** books of hours for noblemen attached to the French Court, were published by the Veuve Cuissary in Paris in 1743, by Benoit Michel Mauteville in Lyon around 1750, and earlier by I. Chardon in Paris in 1682. All of them are about 2 inches high.

A curiously titled German volume of a devotional nature is **Das Buch der Brueder- und Schwesterlichen Bestraffung,** (The Book of Brotherly and Sisterly Punishment). Published by Brinhausser in Augsburg in 1753, it measures 2 by $1\frac{1}{2}$ inches. The only copy of this book we have seen was that sold by Sotheby's at the sale of 22nd July, 1974, belonging to the collection of miniature books of G. J. Sassoon; that collection was in fact part of the famous Vera von Rosenberg library and the above-mentioned book is listed in **Mikrobiblion** under no. 43.

LES JOLIES GAILLARDISES . . . Paris, "Chez les Amis de la Joie", ca. 1800. Frontispiece and Title page.

A fine Jewish prayer book in Spanish for Jews of Sephardic origin was published in the Hague in the year 5494 (i.e. 1732) under the title **Orden de las oraciones quotidianas** (Order of Daily Prayers). The publishers were Selomon de Mercado and Jahacos Castello and the printer C. Hoffeling. The volume has a fine title engraved by D. Coster, 533, (6) pages and measures $2\frac{7}{8}$ by $1\frac{7}{8}$ inches. It is frequently found in beautiful tortoise-shell bindings with chased silver clasps or in finely tooled contemporary morocco.

A delightful miniature prayer book in Hebrew is the **Seder Tefilloth** according to Sephardi rites, printed by Dr. Naphthali Herz Levi in Amsterdam in 1729, size $2\frac{3}{8}$ by $1\frac{9}{16}$ inches. I have seen beautifully bound copies of this scarce volume, one in contemporary painted vellum with attractive Dutch flowered endpapers, another in 18th century black morocco, finely gilt-tooled with leafy borders and built-up centre design with flowers flanking a cornucopia, gauffered edges richly gilt and presented in its original cardboard box. Such splendid condition is usually only found with Hebrew books produced in Holland in the tolerant atmosphere of that country where Jews could lead a more sheltered and less harrassed life than in many other European countries.

Such small devotional works exist in many languages. A German volume, published by Baumann in Breslau in 1725 and measuring $1\frac{9}{16}$ by $\frac{7}{8}$ inches, is entitled **Ein Schönes Gebetbüchlein in allerley Noth und Anliegen zu gebrauchen,** (A Beautiful little Prayer Book to be used in all kinds of Emergencies and Situations). A Swiss devotional work, published in Einsiedeln by Franz Xaver Kälin in 1768, measures $1\frac{13}{16}$ by $1\frac{1}{4}$ inches and bears the flowery title **Lust-Gärtlein einer betrübten Seele täglich zu gebrauchen** (Little Pleasure Garden of a Saddened Soul, for daily use). A concise version of the Gospel of St. John in Flemish, **S. Jans Evangelie,** was published in Antwerp by J. F. de Roveroy Cathyne, ca. 1785, size $1\frac{3}{4}$ by $1\frac{3}{8}$ inches. Besides a half-page title woodcut, it has two interesting cuts, one of the crucifixion, the other portraying the evangelist. Another edition of this rare devotional booklet, also published in Antwerp, has the imprint of J. B. Christiaenssens, *in het Wit Cruys*. It measures 2 by 2 inches. A copy was included in the famous Belgian Van Bever collection. Such books were often carried by simple believing souls as talismans under their shirts at the height of the heart. In any case, the extreme portability of such small prayer books and religious texts assured their owners of mental and spiritual relief and consolation, often far from their homes. The miniature format assumed thus a rôle to which it was peculiarly suited.

SEDER TEFILOTH (Hebrew Prayer Book). Amsterdam, Naphthali Herz Levi, 1739. In contemporary red morocco binding.

CHAPTER FIVE

THUMB BIBLES

When mentioning Weever's **Agnus Dei** and John Taylor's **Verbum Sempiternum** in our chapter on the 17th century, we pointed out that these texts were the predecessors of a large number of similar volumes based on the Old and New Testaments, chiefly intended to appeal to children and young people. Commonly called thumb Bibles because of their small size, they flourished particularly during the eighteenth century although the fashion continued well into the 19th century.

In England, the first of these children's abbreviated Bibles is **Biblia, or a Practical Summary of ye Old & New Testaments,** printed for R. Wilkin in St. Paul's Church Yard, London, 1727 (which date is in many copies altered by hand to 1728). It measures 1⅝ by 1⅛ inches and can be found in beautifully designed black morocco bindings of exceptional quality which one suspects to have been commissioned by the publisher. So far I have seen three almost identical ones, bearing in the centre of both covers a gilt-tooled lozenge within a larger rhombus, surrounded by arabesque and S-shaped tools, double fillets and charming floral corner pieces, richly gilt-tooled spines and with all edges gilt. An engraved title and 16 delightful though simply designed copper plates illustrating highlights of the Bible, make this handy little volume a joy to behold and to possess. The preface begins with the significant sentence: " 't is a Melancholy Reflection that in a country, where all have the Bible in their hands, so many should be ignorant of the first Principles of God". It ends: "The Supreme exercise of the Soul here on Earth, is the pure design of this Treatise, which if read attentively will with God's Assistance answer the Proposed End." This preface is identical with that found in later editions of this thumb Bible and the ten chapters which follow have on the whole remained unaltered.

The "Biblia" makes its next appearance under the title **The Bible in Miniature,** published by W. Harris in London in 1771, 1774 and 1775. All the copies I have seen have had 14 engraved plates and

BIBLIA, OR A PRACTICAL SUMMARY OF YE OLD & NEW TESTAMENTS. London, Wilkin, 1728. Contemporary binding.

33

the sizes were all about $1\frac{5}{8}$ by $1\frac{1}{4}$ inches. Some of these Harris Bibles were, like many of the later Newbery Bibles, finely bound in gilt-tooled red or black morocco, with oval onlays in the centre of both covers bearing in gilt the sacred initials IHS, (Jesus the Saviour of Men).

Much more frequently found are copies of the almost identical **Bible in Miniature,** published in 1780 by Elizabeth Newbery, the widow of Francis Newbery who was the nephew of the famous John Newbery, publisher and author of many pioneering children's books. This family connection is significant, because it partly explains the overwhelming success of that edition. The Newberys with their reputation must have achieved domination of the children's book market of the period. Compared with Wilkin's well conceived issue the later product is distinctly inferior in most respects. The paper is of lower quality, the engravings are often rather worn and even the leather of the externally brilliant trade binding is thinner and more vulnerable.

The majority of copies have no imprint at the end of the text. Rarer issues, however, either bear the imprint "Crowder & Hemsted, Printers, Warwick-Square", or simply "Hemsted, Printer".

Other editions of this thumb Bible, which continued well into the next century, include one printed for J. Harris, late Newbery, and for Darton & Harvey, printed by E. Hemsted, Great-New-Street, London, circa 1790, another one printed by Darton and Harvey around 1802, a **Bible in Miniature, intended as a Present for Youth,** published in Glasgow by Lumsden & Son circa 1800, another edition, "London Printed", dated 1812, another **Bible in Miniature** printed by H. Mozley, in Gainsborough in 1798, 1805, 1808 and 1815, and a later edition, around 1830 by T. & W. McDowell in Edinburgh.

John Bysh published in London, around 1815, **The Holy Bible,** illustrated with 32 copper-engraved plates of considerable quality. It measures $2\frac{13}{16}$ by $1\frac{3}{4}$ inches. The two parts have separate titles, the first **The Juvenile Bible, or History of the**

Old and New Testaments, in Miniature, of 144 pages, the second The Juvenile Testament, or History of the Life of Our Lord and Saviour Jesus Christ, adapted to the capacity of children, of 71 pages. A reprint of the "Biblia" of 1727/8 was issued by Longman & Co. in London in 1857.

The Miniature Bible, or a Practical Summary of ye Old and New Testaments, Dublin, W. Sleater, 1788, measuring $2\frac{1}{4}$ by 2 inches, is one of the earlier Irish miniature books and far from common. It is dedicated to Viscount Wellesley and has two engraved titles. Spielmann, No. 370, points out that the title to the New Testament is significantly altered into ". . . treating of the Evangelical Dispensation by the Ever Blessed Jesus Christ".

American reprints of these children's Bibles often bear the title History of the Bible or Bible History. Under the latter title, an edition was

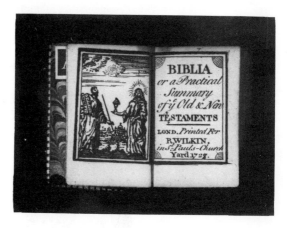

BIBLIA, OR A PRACTICAL SUMMARY OF YE OLD & NEW TESTAMENTS.
London, R. Wilkin, 1728.
Frontispiece and title page. The fore-runner of the Newbery Bible of 1780.

published by S. Wood in New York in 1811, measuring 1¾ by 1⅛ inches. The former title appeared in Boston, Ball and Bedlington, in 1812 and 1814, and in Troy, W. & J. Disturnell, in 1823. H. & E. Phinney published the same History in Cooperstown, New York, from 1829 to 1851 in a number of editions and Phinney & Co. printed that title in Buffalo until at least 1859. An edition printed by J. B. & L. Baldwin in Bridgeport in 1831, 2⅛ by 1¾ inches, reproduces Wilkin's 1727 preface, but has entirely different woodcut illustrations, mainly bold portraits of Old and New Testament characters, including Pontius Pilate. The latest American edition we have seen is a **History of the Bible** printed by Starr & Co. in New London, Connecticut, in 1860.

Similar thumb Bibles came out in Dutch, like the **Biblia, ofte Inhoud des O: en N: Testaments,** with engraved title and 4 plates, published by P. Servaas in The Hague in 1750, size 1⅛ by 15⁄16 inches. German texts include **Biblia, oder Inhalt gantzer Heiliger Schrift,** written by G. C. Ganshorn and issued in Nuremberg by Georg Scheurer in 1705, with four full-page engravings, 1⅜ by 1¹⁄16 inches, which was also published by Jobst Wilhelm Kohles

BIBLE HISTORY. Albany, S. Shaw, ca. 1816. A rare American Thumb Bible.

36

in Altdorff in 1705, measuring $1\frac{3}{8}$ by $\frac{7}{8}$ inches, while the same text, without mentioning Ganshorn's authorship, was published by J. H. Hesse in Halle in 1753 and 1769, with a frontispiece showing a portrait of Martin Luther and the Wartburg, and three other plates, size $1\frac{9}{16}$ by $1\frac{1}{8}$ inches. **Eine kurzgefasste Geschichte der Bibel,** (A brief History of the Bible), intended for German-speaking Americans, was issued by C. Zentler in Philadelphia in 1811. Several French versions include **La Sainte Bible, mis en vers par J.P.J. du Bois,** which came out in The Hague, P. Servaas, in 1752 and 1754, and in Berlin, A. Fromery, 1752, as well as J. Decker, 1762. They all measure about $1\frac{15}{16}$ by $1\frac{3}{8}$ inches. A rare **Sommaire de la Bible,** with woodcut title vignette, woodcut frontispiece and six rather primitive plates, was published by A. de Groot & Fils in the Hague in 1750 and measures $1\frac{7}{8}$ by $1\frac{1}{4}$ inches.

A CONCISE HISTORY OF THE HOLY BIBLE. Liverpool, T. Schofield, 1789. A rare Thumb Bible.

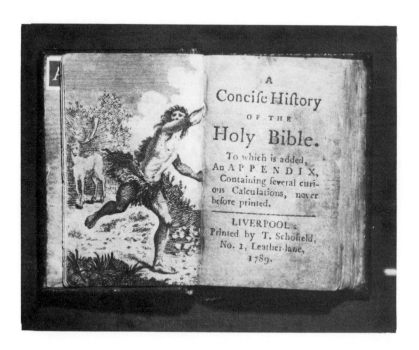

I have just received a copy of **Three Centuries of Thumb Bibles: a Check List** by Ruth Elizabeth Adomeit, published by Garland Publishing, Inc., New York and London, in 1980, listing nearly 300 such items, based on many years of research by that outstanding American miniature book collector. The volume shows clearly the incredible wealth of material available and proves once again that the Bible was and remains the world's most influential book, even in its abbreviated miniature version.

CHAPTER SIX

ENGLISH ALMANACS AND CALENDARS OF THE 18th AND 19th CENTURIES

Almanacs and calendars belong to the most frequently encountered miniature books. By their very nature and ephemeral interest, they were often published in small sizes to ensure that they could be carried in pockets or handbags so as to be ready for instant consultation. In addition, they developed quickly from purely utilitarian objects into decorative and often beautiful gifts. Thus some of the most strikingly attractive miniature books can be found in this category.

The finest examples, especially in England, France, the Netherlands, Germany and Austria, combine all the arts of book-production in an almost perfect manner. Some bibliophiles exclude almanacs from their collections and regard such items as "a-biblia", non-books, but by doing so, they deprive themselves of some of the most handsome and desirable objects in the entire miniature book field. They also overlook the fact that many of these annual volumes are of considerable literary or artistic interest and occasionally contain the first or even only editions of poetry or prose written by well-known authors.

An almanac of small size which appeared continuously for over 200 years, thus establishing a record of longevity in the miniature book world, is the famous **London Almanack,** published by the Company of Stationers. It was preceded for a short period by the **Calendarium Londinense Verum, or Raven's Almanack** of which a copy for the year 1684 was sold at Sotheby's in April, 1979. It has 19 pages and measures $2\frac{3}{16}$ by $\frac{7}{8}$ inches and is engraved throughout. Wing also lists issues for 1678 and 1686. The earliest **London Almanack** proper is that dated 1690, in the British Library. The earliest issue I have personally seen is that of 1713, listed in Spielmann, no. 304, measuring $2\frac{1}{4}$ by $1\frac{1}{16}$ inches. Like all the later editions until the second part of the 19th century, it is engraved throughout. The folding frontispiece does not yet show a London view, but Britannia in her chariot, pulled by a lion and a unicorn. Other early London Almanacks, like that "for the Year of Christ 1729", contain allegorical or symbolical folding plates and mottoes such as "Concord is the cement of publick societies". The earliest with a London view I can recall is that for 1736, showing a splendid panorama of London from the South Bank of the Thames, with London Bridge and its houses to the right, St. Paul's Cathedral near the left-hand corner and including the many spires of the city churches. The almanac of 1737 shows Cripple Gate, Ludgate and Newgate, and Spielmann's second-earliest specimen dating from 1742, has a fine view of the Custom house which like all the earlier engraved frontispieces is not folded and stuck down, but printed on a folding strip.

Other early London views include the Archbishop of Canterbury's Palace at Lambeth (1752), Marlborough House in St. James's Park (1760), Somerset House (1764), Black Friars Bridge (1766), East India House (1768), Westminster Bridge (1769), the New Sessions House (1774), the Adelphi Buildings (1775) and the Ordnance Office, New Palace Yard (1783). In fact, these almanacs provide a fascinating record of London's buildings including a number erected just before publication

LONDON ALMANACK
engraved frontispiece

40

date. The latest London Almanacks I have seen are the ones for 1879, showing Chelsea Embankment; 1882, with the Natural History Museum in Kensington; 1884 the Fishmongers' Hall; 1887, the Chelsea Hospital and 1888, depicting the People's Palace, Mile End. The one for 1896, printed like all the later ones, by letterpress, has no longer any London view for frontispiece. The latest of all the London Almanacks I have seen, is that for 1912.

The size of most of these almanacs is approximately $2\frac{1}{4}$ by $1\frac{1}{4}$ inches, which must be considered the standard format. There exist, however, such almanacs where the leaf is folded horizontally and the book is $1\frac{1}{4}$ inch square; another variation is the curious "finger" format resulting from the leaf being folded vertically with the almanac measuring $2\frac{1}{4}$ by $\frac{5}{8}$ inches, and finally there exists the very rare double-sized almanac of $2\frac{1}{4}$ by $2\frac{5}{8}$ inches. The small-sized square and the finger-sized almanacs have no frontispiece illustrations.

The contents altered little over the years, and are chiefly concerned with the calendar, a table of the reign of British Kings and Queens, details of the current Royal Family, the Cabinet, Lord Mayors and Sheriffs of London, exchange rates (in the earlier issues), stamp duty, transfer days at the bank, high tides, eclipses of sun and moon, etc. The almanacs were published by the Company of Stationers in London, one of the ancient and renowned livery companies of the City, and bear within circular lettering the coat of arms of that august square mile in the heart of London, while a second circular engraving contains the arms of the Stationers' Company, sometimes surrounded by its motto: *Verbum Domini manet in aeternum.*

The almanacs were often issued in stunningly beautiful bindings, with similarly designed slipcases, in shark-skin covered boxes or occasionally with silver or brass clasps. More detailed mention of these is made in the chapter on miniature publishers' bindings.

LONDON ALMANACK, 1870. Characteristic binding.

41

Between 1836 and 1843, there appeared in London a series of all-engraved almanacs of quite exceptional quality, published by Albert Schloss, Fancy Stationer to Her Royal Highness, the Duchess of Kent. For the first three years they were called **The English Bijou Almanac** and from 1839 to 1843 **Schloss's English Bijou Almanac.** They are true miracles of engraving, illustration, binding and presentation. Each of them has six charming plates, almost all of them portraits of famous writers, musicians, painters or stage performers. These portraits are accompanied by poems in praise of the personalities they depict, written by well-known authors of the period. Not infrequently, it is their first appearance in print.

The first of these almanacs, for the year 1836, is also the smallest in size, measuring $\frac{3}{4}$ by $\frac{1}{2}$ of an inch. The poems are by "L.E.L.", Letitia Elizabeth Landon (1802-1838), who after having published a number of novels, amongst them "Ethel Churchill", died tragically from an accidental overdose of prussic acid. The poems concern Lord Byron, the painter Raphael, Schiller, Retzsch, Mrs. Hemans and Martin.

The next two almanacs, for 1837 and 1838, were also "poetically illustrated" by L.E.L. They measure $\frac{13}{16}$ by $\frac{5}{8}$ of an inch. The portraits in the first issue include Coleridge, Goethe, Mrs. Somerville, von Raumer, Cooper and Miss Malibran, the singer and actress. The 1838 edition which, for no particular reason, is more frequently found than either of the preceding almanacs, portrays Queen Victoria, Mozart, Sir Walter Scott, King William IV, Giulia Grisi, the celebrated Italian opera singer, and Letitia Landon herself, to whom a poem by John A. Heraud is dedicated.

The 1839 almanac, still with poems by L.E.L., has portraits of the Duke of Wellington, Sir Thomas Lawrence, Beethoven, the Duchess of Kent, Lady Blessington the novelist, and of the singer Judith Pasta. The 1840 issue, with poems by Samuel Lover (1797-1868), song-writer, novelist and painter, has portraits of the Duchess of

Sutherland, Anna Maria Hall, the popular novelist, W. C. Macready, the famous actor, Martin Archer Shee, the portrait painter, Thomas Moore, the poet, and of Fanny Persiani. The poems in the 1841 edition are by the Hon. Mrs. Norton (1808-1877), poetess and social reformer. The portraits include Napoleon, Sheridan Knowles, Princess Marie of Hesse, Mrs. Norton and Marie Taglioni, the celebrated dancer. There is also an engraved view of Caernarvon Castle. The 1842 almanac, again with poems by Mrs. Norton, has portraits of the Princess Royal, Ellen Tree (Mrs. Kean), the actress, Mlle. Rachel, the great French actress, John Murray, Herr Staudigl, and of Charles Dickens, whose smallest known portrait this is.

The last **Schloss's Bijou Almanac** is of particular interest, as its literary contributions are written by the famous Mary Russell Mitford, authoress of **Our Village.** The portraits depict the King of Prussia, the Duchess of Orleans, the Prince of Wales, Samuel Rogers, Ludwig Dobler and Adelaide Kemble, a singer and author and daughter of the great actor.

The size of all these almanacs is minute, around $\frac{13}{16}$ by $\frac{9}{16}$ of an inch. The quality of the engraving is of the highest order and is due to the great skill of Benjamin Rees Davies who had been active since about 1820. Iain Bain writes in his fine book specially devoted to the Schloss almanacs: "Davies's work is the equivalent of 3 point or less. The consistency of his skill and the remarkable excellence of the tiny portraiture emphasizes his unusual combination of talents."

To such outstanding achievements in the field of engraving must be added the great care which has been lavished on the presentation of these almanacs. They are usually found in most attractive finely gilt-tooled glazed boards or leathers of delicate colours, with gilt edges, and often preserved in fine fitted jewel cases, covered with morocco leather or velvet, each also containing a tiny and elegant magnifying glass. No wonder that Schloss, in his advertisements, draws attention to

43

the fact that his establishment was "patronised by Her Majesty the Queen and all the Royal Family." Some of the more exalted examples are described in the chapter on publishers' bindings.

Less refined, but still possessed of great charm and quality, are the **Bijou Almanacks** published in London by D. Bogue, T. Goode, Rock Brothers or Rock Brothers and Payne between 1845 and 1856. Most of them are, like Schloss's marvels, engraved throughout and vary in size between 1 by $\frac{5}{8}$ inches and $1\frac{1}{8}$ by $\frac{3}{4}$ inches. The almanacs with the Bogue imprint were frequently issued for the same years as those of T. Goode, but are superior to them in workmanship and general quality. Some of these volumes were produced by lithography. The illustrations show portraits of rulers and statesmen, biblical figures, views of buildings or landscapes, etc. The **Bijou Almanack** for 1851 issued by D. Bogue is of special theatrical interest with portraits of Jenny Lind, Fanny Elster, Taglioni and Carlotta Grisi, while the almanac for 1852, produced by Rock Brothers and Payne has well-designed views of Washington, St. Petersburg, Rome, Constantinople, Lisbon, Madrid, Vienna and Brussels. Most of the almanacs are bound either in richly gilt-stamped boards or similarly decorated flexible morocco.

Many collectors also value highly another series issued under the title **Tilt's Miniature Almanack** or **Tilt's Useful Almanack** by one or the other of the following publishers: Charles Tilt, Tilt and Bogue, D. Bogue, late Tilt and Bogue, W. Kent, Piper and Carter and Kent & Co. over a period ranging from 1836 to at least 1886. They all measure approximately $2\frac{3}{8}$ by $1\frac{3}{8}$ inches and contain similar information to that found in the **London Almanacks,** i.e. a calendar, details about the Royal Family, European Kings and Queens, ministers of the Crown, bishops, bankers, etc. The bindings vary from publisher's roan with flap to close, to coloured morocco in slipcases; most frequently the Tilt almanacs are bound in rather unimpressive gilt-stamped flexible green cloth.

The Victoria Miniature Almanack, starting in the early 1840's has from the 1846 issue onwards a rather amusing additional title **Fashionable Remembrancer.** All the issues we have seen are printed by R. Allen of Nottingham, even as late as 1880, while the publishers vary from W. Strange, London (at least up to 1852) to Kent & Co., London, and finally to E. W. Allen, London. The size of all these almanacs is approximately $2\frac{1}{2}$ by $1\frac{3}{8}$ inches. They are nicely produced and the interesting contents include in 1845 poems by Longfellow, Frances Brown and Kenworthy as well as short prose essays; the 1846 volume contains a ballroom guide and an essay on Newstead Abbey; in 1847 we find also a "language of flowers"; 1848 has facetious short tales, a poem by 'Crowquill', the ballroom guide and a description of Donnington Hall, while 1849 has useful statistics and information, various anecdotes and aphorisms, a poem by Chas. Swain and other features. The illustrations are mostly lithographed, some in gold, and include views, a charming ball scene (in 1846), young people dancing on a village green (1847), the last moments of the Duke of Wellington (1854), Windsor Castle and Queen Victoria with her Consort (1855), etc.

The British Library have in their miniature book collection quite a few issues of **The Royal Miniature Almanack,** published by T. Goode in London from their address at Aylesbury Street. Five of the issues, those for 1854, 1857, 1858, 1859 and 1861 are bound together in two very regal looking volumes in red morocco with a gilt-stamped crown on the spines. They measure $1\frac{3}{4}$ by $1\frac{1}{4}$ inches. I have also seen earlier issues like those for 1846, 1848 and 1852. Most of them contain portraits of Queen Victoria, Prince Albert or other members of the Royal family. The quality of these illustrations is however not very high. The almanacs were issued in black wrappers, like most of Goode's prolific output of miniature ephemera.

The last series of English almanacs we would like to mention is **De La Rue's improved condensed Diary and Engagement Book** of whjch we have seen various issues between 1880 and 1901. Most of them are in the unusual "finger shape" and are specifically described as such on their title pages. They measure 3 by $\frac{7}{8}$ inches and are bound in black or red finely gilt-stamped morocco in similar slipcases. The edges are gilt and they are printed in red and blue. A much rarer format, described by the publishers, the famous firm of De La Rue in London, as "Thumb Shape", measures $1\frac{3}{4}$ by $1\frac{1}{2}$ inches and is found in red morocco binding with gilt fillets and flap to close. The contents are stated to have been edited by William Godward, late of the **Nautical Almanac** office and contain diary pages which are blank except for the date, day of the week and feast days, also including indications like "Last day pay fire in", "Midsummer Day", "Half-Quarter Day", etc. The main information at the beginning includes law sittings, university terms, holidays at public offices, eclipses, inland postal rates, and so on. Occasionally these well-printed almanacs have interesting advertisements at the end, such as the "Pelican Self-Feeding Pen" and the "Swift Reservoir Penholder", describing these early fountain pens.

LE REVEIL MATIN ALMANACH. Paris, 1783. In case.

CHAPTER SEVEN

FRENCH, GERMAN, AUSTRIAN, DUTCH AND OTHER EUROPEAN ALMANACS

France is perhaps the country where the art of the almanac reached its highest peak. A significant proportion of these publications were produced in miniature format and often reduced to such small sizes that they are now classified as *almanachs microscopiques*.

Gaston Tissandier in his **Livres Minuscules** has described, though not catalogued in detail, the finest collection of its kind, that of Georges Salomon of Paris which later passed on to Arthur A. Houghton and was sold with his miniature library at Christie's December 1979 auction. Although the Salomon collection was by no means confined to almanacs, it contained more and finer examples of these little treasures than could be assembled by a present-day collector anywhere.

Of particular rarity are some of the slightly larger volumes listed in the Houghton Sale catalogue under no. 89. That part of the collection comprised 26 volumes published between 1790 and 1814 by Jubert, Janet, Marcilly or Le Fuel in Paris. They all have engraved titles and most of them contain twelve full-page plates executed with the greatest care and delicacy, representing elegant scenes of contemporary life, frequently including entrancing pictures of courting couples. Most of the almanacs measure approximately $2\frac{9}{16}$ by $1\frac{13}{16}$ inches and their titles are: **Le Calendrier de Minerve, L'École de la Modestie, Les Tableaux de l'Expérience, Les Délices de l'Adolescence, Les Bucoliques de Cythère, Les Leçons Pastorales, Les Charmes de la Sensibilité, Les Étrennes de l'Age d'Or, Le Charmant Petit Confident, Les Échos des Bocages, Les Douceurs de la Nature, Le Triomphe de l'Esprit, Les Plaisirs Purs, Le Sentiment Analysé, Le Passe-Tems de tous les Ages, Étrennes sans Pareilles, Les Beaux Caprices d'un Jeune poète, Mes Rêveries, Le Petit Page, Les Fêtes du Hameau, La Fleur des Champs,** and **Étrennes de Minerve.** A few of the titles reappear in different years. The finely illustrated bibliography by Grand-Carteret **Les Almanachs Français**

48

Original decorative bindings of French miniature almanacs of the late 18th and early 19th centuries.

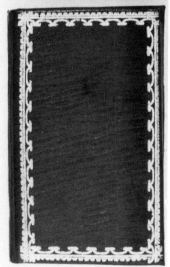

describes most of these so floridly and charmingly titled volumes in great detail and illustrates some of the finest. Plate 7 in Christie's Catalogue of the Houghton miniature books reproduces some of the splendid bindings in beautifully tooled morocco or elaborate needlework. Collectors who succeed in finding any of these magnificent almanacs all of which are now exceedingly rare, must deem themselves very fortunate.

It is a strange phenomenon that the large number of smaller almanacs published in Paris during the 18th and 19th century have survived much more frequently than the more substantial ones we have just described. All of them are engraved throughout and illustrated with lovely full-page plates. They measure between $\frac{7}{8}$ by $\frac{11}{16}$ and $1\frac{1}{8}$ by $\frac{3}{4}$ inches, a very small format indeed. Most of the copies are bound in contemporary morocco, the majority coloured red or maroon, but they are also found in green, olive, or black leathers while a few were much more elaborately produced in jewelled bindings.

These "microscopic" almanacs began to appear around the 1760's. Mainly intended as presents for ladies or young people, they were often distributed by chocolate shops, pastry cooks, etc. as New Year presents to their best clients. The earliest of these tiny volumes we have seen is **La Bagatelle du Jour, Étrennes portatif** for 1767, engraved by Cocquelle, with five hand-coloured illustrations, showing elegant young ladies besieged by Cupids, published by *un limonadier,* a seller of lemonade, which is listed in the Houghton Catalogue, no. 13 and described in greater detail in my Catalogue 91, item 10. Castaing, in his list of miniature French almanacs, states that six of them were published between 1765 and 1784, nineteen between 1789 and 1803, thirty-nine between 1816 and 1830, and thirteen between 1831 and 1850.

That particular list is restricted to almanacs in the 128mo format and is by no means complete. As can be seen, it is very brief for almanacs published before the French Revolution and includes three other volumes engraved by Cocquelle, the **Almanach Nouveau Portatif** for 1765, **Le Reveille-Matin,** 1766, and **Le Bijou Mignon des Dames,** 1769. The second of these titles is of particular interest with its twelve engravings representing street cries of Paris. It is surprising that publication of these little luxury objects continued during the revolutionary period. At least one of them, **Les Étrennes Nationales à l'usage des Dames Patriotes,** does in its illustrations and song texts pay heed to the prevailing revolutionary mood. It was published by Blanmayeur in 1793. Most of the almanacs issued during the following years bear the imprint of Jubert, Janet, Marcilly or Le Fuel. They all contain songs and fine engraved plates illustrating the texts and are occasionally accompanied by their music. They comprise 64 pages, including the obligatory calendar. Their titles are a reflection of their delightful contents, for example **Amour et Amitié, Bijou des Dames, L'Apropos Galant, Le Conseiller des Graces, Le Petit Bijou des Enfans, Le Petit Menestrel, Les Curieux Précoces, Les Petits Montagnards, Valeur et Constance, Les Doux Liens de Famille, Les Jeux de l'Amour, Plaisir et Gaité, Voici vos Étrennes,** and many similar imaginative and suggestive headings.

Of great rarity is the all-engraved pictorial **Calendrier de tous les Saints,** comprising twelve monthly volumes depicting the Saints for each day of the year. These tiny tomes, measuring $\frac{3}{4}$ by $\frac{5}{8}$ of an inch, were published without imprint about 1815 or earlier and obviously originate in France. The Houghton Catalogue, nos. 49 and 50, lists one complete and one incomplete set of this beautiful miniature work which is so elusive that we had previously over a period of thirty years seen only one single volume, that for **février.**

Many almanacs of great quality and beauty appeared in the German language, chiefly in Germany and Austria, some of them of very small size. The **Hand Calender auf das Jahr Jesu Christi 1775,** engraved throughout and printed in red and black, was one of the items comprising no. 3 in Christie's Houghton Sale catalogue and is one of the earlier German almanacs of particular quality and originality. It was published by Johann Georg Schreibers seel. Wittwe (the widow of J. G. Schreiber) in Leipzig and measures $1\frac{13}{16}$ by $\frac{5}{8}$ inches. The well-engraved frontispiece shows a jolly portrait of Friedrich August, Elector of Saxony. Each month is headed by an attractive oblong vignette with scenes of domestic and agricultural life. The volume contains currency conversion tables and illustrations of the signs of the zodiac. Bound in pink silk, it is preserved in its original gilt-tooled calf-leather case. A **Wahrhafter immer-währender Calender** (A Truly Everlasting Calendar), was published by Matthäus Albrecht Lotter in Augsburg in 1776, measuring $2\frac{1}{2}$ by $1\frac{13}{16}$ inches. The **Wiener-Kalenderl** 1765, printed in black and red, with twelve lively engravings of tavern scenes, was published by August Schatten in Vienna. In the same city appeared **Neuer Krakauer verfertigter Finger-Kalender** 1795, issued by the nobleman Joh. Thom. Edler von Trattnern and measuring $2\frac{7}{8}$ by $1\frac{3}{16}$ inches. It gives information on noble births, postal charges and the value of gold coins. Quite a few almanacs mention the city of Cracow in their title although they were published in Vienna. The issue for 1805, also due to von Trattnern, exists in hand-painted enamel covers with a mirror inside the front-cover. In 1793, a **Wiener Kalenderl,** a little Viennese calendar came out, published by the heirs of the Edlen von Ghelen, printed in red and black and measuring $2\frac{3}{4}$ by $1\frac{1}{16}$ inches. **Fingerl-Kalender auf das Jahr 1807** appeared in Brünn (now Brno, Czechoslovakia) under the imprint of Joseph Georg Trassler. Measuring $2\frac{13}{16}$ by $1\frac{3}{16}$ inches, it can be found in most attractively hand-painted enamelled covers, showing a woman on the upper and a man on the lower cover, both in colourful costume.

A **Mignon-Almanach** with 13 or 14 calligraphically engraved leaves was published over a prolonged period by Joseph Riedl in Vienna. The earliest issue we find recorded is that of 1813, measuring an oblong $\frac{3}{4}$ by $1\frac{1}{8}$ inches, the 1815 editon measures $\frac{1}{2}$ by $1\frac{1}{8}$ inches and that for 1816 about the same. Riedl also published **Der allerkleinste Favorit-Kalender** (The Smallest-ever Favourite Calendar). The 1819 edition had 14 printed leaves and measures $1\frac{9}{16}$ by $\frac{13}{16}$ inches, while the 1823 issue has 25 leaves, including eleven full-page illustrations of allegorical character, size $1\frac{5}{8}$ by $\frac{7}{8}$ inches. A **Mignon Almanach** published by Fr. Riedl's sel. Witwe und Sohn was published as late as 1850 and measures $1\frac{3}{8}$ by $\frac{7}{8}$ inches. A **Trachten-Almanach,** (A Costume Almanac), for the year 1840 was issued by the same publishers in Vienna printed in black and red and bound in colourfully embossed golden wrappers, measuring $2\frac{11}{16}$ by $1\frac{13}{16}$ inches. It has a charming engraved title and seven hand-coloured costume

WIENER-KALENDER AUF DAS JAHR 1814. Vienna, Jos. Riedl. Original enamelled covers painted by hand.

plates, each showing a couple from one of the Austro-Hungarian provinces. A similar almanac **Taschen-Kalender,** pocket calendar of miniature size was issued by the Königlich Preussische Kalender Deputation in 1830 and contained twelve costume engravings by Riepenhausen depicting Polish, Silesian, Moravian, Carinthian, Hungarian and Siebenbürgen couples.

The most interesting German-language almanacs are perhaps the tiny volumes produced by lithography by C. F. Müller in Karlsruhe and by Clemens or Alois Senefelder in Munich. The latter was the inventor of lithography and the earliest of these **Almanach** issues, published between the years 1817 and circa 1840 are certainly considered and eagerly collected as *incunabula* of the art of lithography. As their height varies between only $\frac{11}{16}$ and $\frac{7}{8}$ of an inch by a width of $\frac{7}{16}$ to $\frac{5}{8}$ of an inch, thus making them minute creations, they must be

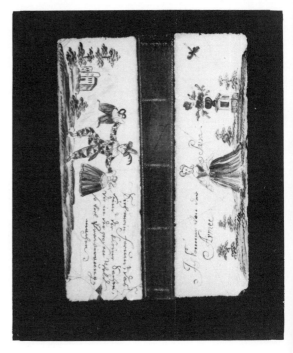

WIENNER-KALENDERL
1765. Vienna, Aug. Schatten.
Original curious enamelled
covers in green, red, blue and
yellow.

54

considered technical miracles of the first order. In addition, the illustrations are often very well designed and executed in great detail. The almanacs were mostly issued in green or pink wrappers and preserved in slipcases. Being so very small and thin and easily mislaid or lost, they have for a long time been very rare. It may be many years before another large batch of them like that listed in the Houghton Sale Catalogue under nos. 9 and 10 will come onto the market. Together with Schloss's Bijous and the tiny engraved French almanacs they rank amongst the most desirable miniature books and are much coveted by collectors.

The last amongst the many German calendars and almanacs we would like to mention are those published nearly a hundred years later by Carl Fromme in Vienna and called **Fromme's Wiener Portemonnaie Kalender** or **Fromme's Rokoko Kalender.** Published between circa 1894 and 1934 and measuring approximately 2 by $1\frac{3}{8}$ inches, they are remarkable for their extraordinary and highly inventive publisher's bindings, described in the chapter devoted to such bindings.

Amongst the almanacs printed in the Netherlands, the very finely produced **De Kleine Tijdwijzer, of Jufferlijke Almanach** is outstan-

HAND KALENDER. Leipzig, 1775.

55

dingly attractive. It was published over a number of years, by J. van Gulik in Amsterdam. We have seen the editions for 1781, 1784 and 1793, listed in Houghton under No. 74, as well as that for 1796 with its six charming double-page engravings showing domestic or amorous scenes and containing short stories and poems. They all measure approximately $2\frac{5}{8}$ by $1\frac{5}{16}$ inches and can be found in gorgeous bindings of painted or gilt-tooled moroccos, mother-of-pearl and other materials.

An unusual almanac, the **Kalender 1753** was printed by the children of Salomon Propes in Amsterdam, size $3\frac{3}{8}$ by $1\frac{3}{8}$ inches, containing a chronicle of Jewish history in Hebrew and details about freight ships, postal services, markets, etc. in Yiddish.

In conclusion it must be stressed that this chapter on almanacs and calendars is very selective, as a great number of miniature books were published in this ephemeral field. It leaves considerable leeway to the collector who will be able to add the joys of discovery to his pleasure of possession.

CHAPTER EIGHT

THE 19th CENTURY, THE SUPREME AGE OF THE MINIATURE BOOK

During the nineteenth century an almost incredible expansion took place in the popularity of miniature books, their subjects extending into many fields, and at the same time technological advances exercised increasing influence on their production. The invention of lithography, already mentioned in the preceding chapter, coupled with that of photography, brought about splendid advances in the field of book production which benefited miniature volumes in a very special way. The marriage of lithography and photography made possible the creation of tiny volumes by the simple process of reduction, as exemplified by many of those published by Bryce in Glasgow. Thus photolithography and photozincography have opened the way to entirely new types of miniature books, which were simply copies of already existing larger volumes.

Simultaneously, some typefounders of great skill and inventiveness provided the means of creating books compressed into the smallest possible compass without any loss of quality, but on the contrary often gaining a charm and beauty hitherto undreamt of.

Equally, the advance of an interest in general education helped the production of many finely illustrated books specially intended for children and young people. The great national literatures of past and present, plays, novels, poetry and essays, became available to miniature book readers and collectors, to be perused, cherished and carried about. In a century which witnessed a strong religious revival and the building of many new churches, prayer books and other devotional texts were printed in their millions and were frequently either created as or transformed into very small and eminently portable volumes.

The industrial revolution, coupled with an unprecedented growth in the means of communication, railways and postal services, had their stimulating effect on every aspect of life, including of course the manufacture and distribution of miniature books. Towards the end of the century they were often sent to relations and friends as Christmas or birthday presents and became valued and occasionally valuable travelling companions in a more mobile age.

We have already singled out two categories of miniature books for treatment in separate chapters. In view of the enormous number of tiny volumes produced after 1800, it becomes necessary to group the most notable subjects into separate articles, and include in them books published up to and including the First World War.

CHAPTER NINE

ENGLISH CHILDREN'S BOOKS AFTER 1800

The very first years of the nineteenth century enriched the world of miniature books in a most striking way. Around 1800 several London publishers and especially John Marshall, a printer and bookseller, and John Harris, successor to the famous Newbery family business, brought out complete libraries for children of great appeal which were housed in their own specially designed ornamental bookcases.

The most enchanting of them is **The Infant's Library** in 16 volumes, published by John Marshall in London around 1800 and reprinted in dated editions in 1819 and 1821. Each volume measures $2\frac{1}{4}$ by $1\frac{7}{8}$ inches and is bound in boards of various pastel shades, pink, green, fawn and grey, with oval or star-shaped coloured paper labels on both covers. The volumes are ensconced in a special bookcase divided into four compartments lined with pink paper. The outstanding feature is the attractive sliding lid covering the front and showing in its turn a nicely painted bookcase in red and green. The engraved label affixed to the back reads: "The Infant's Library, Made and Sold by John Marshall, Printer and Bookseller, No. 4, Aldermary Church Yard, London, where may be had a great variety of books and schemes for the instruction and amusement of young people".

Both my dear old customer the late Sidney Roscoe in *The Book Collector*, Summer 1955, and the Spielmann Catalogue, no. 209, describe in considerable detail the delightful volumes, all but two of which are charmingly illustrated. Of particular interest are Book One with a woodcut picture alphabet, Book 7 with 13 lovely etchings of flowers, Book 9 with 13 interesting pictures of boys' games and Book 13 depicting the same number of girls' games. Amongst these are blindman's buff, hunt-the-slipper, hop-hat, leap-frog, flying kites, cricket, etc. As to swinging on the swings, this is declared "very improper for young ladies". The other volumes in **The Infant's Library** illustrate objects of daily use, rural scenes, ice-skating, ships, a castle, a shooting scene, etc. The only unillustrated volume is Book 2, a rather uninspiring spelling book. The unnumbered Book 16 is "A short history of England" with 34 circular woodcut portraits of the English sovereigns up to and including George III and Queen Charlotte. Roscoe mentions several variants and also refers to an 1819 edition, while we have seen the 1821 edition with plates issued by the publishers in colour. At that time the firm was located at 140 Fleet Street.

There exists a version of **The Infant's Library** in French and we have also heard of an edition in German. Marshall also published **The Child's Latin Library,** with Latin text, a set of this is in the famous miniature library of Irene Winterstein. In that version of great rarity, a bird in a cage becomes "avis intro caveam"; infants in those far-off days must have been very learned indeed.

These various editions were quite reasonably priced but even so the English version of the set in its original bookcase priced at six shillings can only have been accessible to the wealthier parents. To-day the cost of these coveted miniature volumes is several hundred times that amount.

John Marshall published a sequel to this library in 1801, calling it **The Infant's Cabinet of various Objects.** It comprises two volumes of 30 pages each, accompanied by 28 charming engraved cards, with hand-coloured pictures of a sun-dial, tents, a milkwoman, a dancing bear, a puppet show, young archers, a match boy, a stage coach, etc. The books are bound in boards, one in yellow the other in blue, decorated with oval labels inscribed "Various Objects". They measure $1\frac{7}{8}$ by $1\frac{5}{8}$ inches while the size of the cards is $2\frac{3}{4}$ by $1\frac{7}{8}$ inches. The collection is housed in its original wooden box with a coloured and varnished lid showing a mother with her little boy and girl. The box measures $3\frac{5}{8}$ by $2\frac{1}{2}$ by $1\frac{1}{2}$ inches. Such an item, with its loose cards, can only have survived by a miracle for 180 years. It is therefore not surprising that we have seen only one complete copy of this delightful, entertaining and instructive miniature item for small children which in design and typography is strongly reminiscent of

The Infant's Library.

Indefatigable in his efforts to provide the very best and most enchanting books for his youngest readers, John Marshall published in ca. 1802 **The Infant's Cabinet of the Cries of London,** again two volumes and 28 engraved and hand-coloured cards, of the same size as the previously mentioned item, the actual cabinet also of the same proportions, the hand-painted sliding lid showing a London street scene. Gumuchian, No. 1942, calls this entrancing set one of the rarest "Cries of London".

Further juvenilia issued by Marshall include **The Infant's Path Strewed with Flowers,** a reward book of 81 pages, measuring $2\frac{11}{16}$ by $2\frac{1}{16}$ inches, and a similar volume, **The Child's Cabinet. Arrangement of the Birds, Beasts and Insects in the Reward Box** of 77 pages, size 3 by $2\frac{3}{16}$ inches, which both appeared around 1800 and are attractively bound in contemporary Dutch flowered boards.

The **Cabinet of Lilliput,** another most desirable complete library for slightly older children, was published by J. Harris, Successor to E. Newbery in London in 1802. It consists of 12 volumes bound in pink, orange, yellow, green or grey boards, each comprising just over 90 pages and measuring $2\frac{3}{4}$ by $2\frac{11}{16}$ inches. The library is kept in its original wooden book case, with shelving in four sections. The sliding lid shows a very pretty coloured picture of a winged angel teaching children. It is lettered "The Cabinet of Lilliput, Stored with Instruction and Delight" and measures circa 6 by $3\frac{1}{2}$ inches

Each volume contains two or three "instructive stories" and has a fine engraved frontispiece. The stories are: The Spoilt Children; The Disinterested Arab, and Conceit; The Utility of Commerce, Theresa, and The Gardener & Nightingale; Tom Restless, and The History of Theodore; Shadrach the Jew, Maurice, and The Advantages of Industry; Rashness, Alonzo, and Indolence Reclaimed; Jacob the Fisherman, Adelaide, and Little Martin; The Workbag, Charles and his little Poney, and The Story of Mary-Ann; Juliet, and Emmeline; Arthur, and George; Patty, and Janet; Jenny and Edgar, and Florentine; Julia and the Dog, Good Behaviour to Servants, Industry and the Ant. Gumuchian, no. 998 describes the collection as "very rare". It is a pleasing feature of these volumes that they do indeed, as the title on the beautiful bookcase indicates, combine instruction with delight and must have filled their young owners with happiness and pride, enhanced still further because of their miniature format.

In the same year of 1802, and partly during the previous year, an unusually small and textually fascinating series of children's books made its appearance in London, published by R. Snagg and printed by Evans and Ruffy. Amusingly and with deliberate inconsistency, they were described as **Lilliputian Folio Editions.** They measure approximately $1\frac{1}{2}$ by $1\frac{1}{8}$ inches, are bound in boards of different colours and issued in a slipcase. Because of their tiny size and perhaps also due to their unusually absorbing contents, very few copies have survived; most of them must have been lost or read to shreds. They contain much more text than is at a first glance apparent, as the ingenious publisher has consistently used many contractions and abbreviations. In his "address to youth" he describes these tomes as "literary toys".

Spielmann nos. 353A and 471B lists two of the editions, **A Description of the City of London,** 1802, of 117 pages, which is the first half of **The Lilliputian Historian** and continued by **Description of the City of Westminster** which brings the work up to 218 pages, and his second title is **Gulliver's Travels, containing his Voyages to Lilliput, etc.,** 1801, of 120 pages.

While these two volumes are the only ones I have personally seen and handled, *Miniature Book News,* No. 32, also mentions **The Famous History of Valentine and Orson** 1801, with 122 pages, **The History of the Seven Champions of Christendom,** 1801, with 122 pages, **A Description of England and Wales,** 1802, 122 pages, **The History of England: From Jul. Caesar to**

George III, 1802, with 122 pages, and finally **The History of the Holy Bible** of 1802. Dawson's Book Shop, Los Angeles, in their splendid Catalogue 444, compiled by Ruth Adomeit, give more titles in this series, all dated 1801, i.e. **The History of R. Crusoe, of York, Mariner, Pilpay's Fables** and **Fairy Tales,** all having 122 pages.

These volumes were also offered together in their original book-shaped box lettered "Pocket Library of Lilliputian Folio Books".

Only a few years later, Darton, Harvey and Darton & J. Harris published a series of children's books illustrated with engravings designed by Alfred Mills. The first to appear was **A Short History of the Bible and Testament,** dated Oct. 10, 1807, with 48 "neat engravings" of excellent quality, measuring $2\frac{1}{4}$ by $2\frac{1}{8}$ inches, an almost square format like all the volumes in this series. These London printed volumes became immensely popular and are much loved by children to this very day. They were issued in pink boards with the title and price printed on the front-cover and a list of the other available titles on the lower cover. These copies were priced one shilling and sixpence while those bound in red or green roan were priced two shillings.

The sizes vary slightly from copy to copy, the first volume in this delightful and homely series being the smallest; we have seen reprints of it dated 1810, measuring $2\frac{3}{8}$ by $2\frac{5}{16}$ inches, a copy of the 1811 edition measuring a square $2\frac{3}{8}$ by $2\frac{3}{8}$ inches, while yet another issue dated 1812 measures $2\frac{1}{2}$ by $2\frac{3}{8}$ inches. Each volume has 96 pages as have all the other volumes illustrated by Mills. **Pictures of Roman History in Miniature, with Explanatory Anecdotes** was published in 1809, 1812 and 1817; **Pictures of Grecian History, in Miniature** appeared in 1810 and 1812, **Pictures of English History in Miniature, with Descriptions,** a two volume set with 96 engraved plates, was published in 1811, 1815 and as late as 1824. **Natural History of 48 Quadrupeds** was issued in 1810 and 1815, **Natural History of 48 Birds** in 1812 and 1816,

Pictures

OF

GRECIAN HISTORY,

IN MINIATURE,

Designed by ALFRED MILLS.

WITH

DESCRIPTIONS.

London : Printed for Harvey and Darton,
Gracechurch-street;

And J. Harris, St. Paul s Church-yard.

1825.

*Locrquis presenting his brothers child to
Kinz*

A

*PICTURES OF GRECIAN
HISTORY IN MINIATURE
... by Alfred Mills. London,
Harvey and Darton, 1825.*

33

DR. FRANKLIN.

Dr. Franklin was born in
America. He was a poor printer's boy, with no friend to take
care of him, or provide him with
food or clothes; in short, he had
nothing but what he worked for,
yet he found time to improve
himself when his work was done.
He rose early and lived sparing-
ly, that he might save money to
buy books. He read at every

E

BENJ. FRANKLIN LL.D. F.R.S.
born 1706 — died 1790.

*BIOGRAPHY OF EMINENT
PERSONS. London, Mills,
1814.*

64

each of these titles with 48 plates. **Biography of Eminent Persons, alphabetically arranged** was published in 1814 with 47 plates of engraved portraits including those of Captain Cook, Mungo Park, Dr. Johnson, William Penn, Benjamin Franklin, Newton and Linnaeus. There followed in 1814 and again in 1818 **London in Miniature,** "with engravings of its public buildings and antiquities", with 48 good London views. Also in 1814 **Costumes of different Nations, in Miniature** made its appearance, with 47 curious plates including a Chinese vendor of puppies and rats intended for meat pies. The last of the Mills volumes is **Portraits of the Sovereigns of England from Egbert to the Present Time** with 47 circular portraits, which came out in 1817 and 1825.

Some of the books in this series can be found in a later edition, with the date on the title erased and bound in red cloth, stamped in gilt and blind.

Several editions of Mills were published in the United States of America. In Philadelphia, the **Short History of the Bible and Testament** appeared with the imprint of Johnson and Warner as early as in 1809. In New York, Samuel Wood and Sons, Pelsue and Gould, later Gould and Van Pelt, as well as Wm. B. Gilley brought out Mills editions, as did Cooke and Hale in Hartford, Connecticut. All these editions were in size and general character closely fashioned on the English examples.

The French were less scrupulous in producing imitations of the Mills series and Mr. Julian Edison, the editor of *Miniature Book News,* points out that some of the engravings were reproduced in reverse which is evidence that they were not printed from the original plates but copied mechanically. French sets were issued by F. Denn, Giraldon-Bovinet and Alexis Eymery in Paris, but the earliest examples known to us were those published in that city by Guyot et de Pelafol who issued a **Bible de l'Enfance** in 1815, measuring $2\frac{5}{8}$ by $2\frac{3}{8}$ inches and the **Histoire Naturelle de 48**

Oiseaux in 1816, followed during the same year by the French versions of the Pictures of Greek and Roman History. Some of these French sets contain additional titles like a two-volume set **Tableaux de l'Histoire de France** and a **Tableaux de l'Histoire des Juifs,** issued by Eymery in 1826. That edition, with a height of $3\frac{1}{2}$ inches, exceeds our size limit and is only quoted to show the influence these well conceived juvenilia had in other lands. Even a Swedish edition of the **Roman History for Children** has come to our notice, published in 1824 by the Ecksteinska Printing House in Stockholm and measuring $2\frac{9}{16}$ by 2 inches.

Mills made a very definite and valuable contribution to the popularisation of miniature books. These squat and handy volumes with their entertaining as well as instructive contents did capture the imagination of countless children. Handwritten inscriptions and dedications on endpapers and flyleaves testify to their enduring popularity amongst generations of young people. To this day they are eagerly sought after by minibibliophiles which fact explains the steady rise in the price they fetch at auctions.

Charles Tilt (1797-1861) whose miniature almanacs we have already mentioned, has also made an excellent miniature contribution in the juvenile field. Under the collective title of "Tilt's Hand-Books for Children" he issued a series of particularly attractive volumes, many of them devoted to various aspects of natural history, all of them bound in gilt-stamped cloth with gilt edges and measuring 3 by $2\frac{1}{2}$ inches. They are undated but were published around 1835. They are all illustrated with 48 pretty woodcut plates and comprise approximately 192 pages each. Very occasionally they are found in their own specially manufactured cardboard bookcase covered in leather bearing in front in gilt lettering within arabesque decorations the inscription "My Own Library".

Two titles, **The Little Book of British Birds** and **The Little Book of British Quadrupeds** were written by W. May, while Charles Williams is the author of **The Zoological Gardens, Regent's Park** and **The Surrey Zoological Gardens.** Much sought after by collectors are **The Little Robinson Crusoe** and **The Little Esop,** published like the following title, **Famous Men of Britain** by Tilt and Bogue. Osborne I, 164, dates the latter volume as circa 1841. It includes biographies and portraits of the Venerable Bede, Bacon, Robert Boyle, James Watt, Captain Cook and others. Other volumes in this series are **The Little Picture Bible** and **The Little Picture Testament,** both written by Isabella Child, a **Little History of England,** and **Country Walks for Little Folks** of which Gumuchian, no. 1898 praises the "tiny woodcuts, admirably executed". Lastly Tilt was responsible for a volume of particular London interest, **London Sights for Little Folks** which illustrates amongst other subjects school-girls of the Blue-Coat School, a children's Guy Fawkes procession, a steam gun, paving workers, an advertising caravan, and placard bearers.

Tilt's miniatures also exist in an American version, published by Smith & Peck in Philadelphia in 1844. They are more or less identical with the English edition in text, illustrations and size. Loomis & Peck published some additional volumes in 1845 and 1847, including Child's **Natural History of Fishes** and specifically American titles, **Little History of the United States, Famous Men of the United States,** etc. which are the equivalent of two titles referred to above.

While Tilt's Handbooks cannot be described as rare and many copies have come my way over the years, their apparently everlasting popularity has resulted in making it increasingly difficult to find fine and complete copies of these pleasing little volumes.

Towards the end of the 19th century and the early nineteen hundreds, the London publishers Wells Gardner, Darton & Co. brought out **The Midget Series,** measuring 3 by $2\frac{1}{2}$ inches, bound in "fancy boards" or very rarely in "fancy calf", with gilt edges. In their publicity, the publishers commend "these tiny volumes" and add that they "will be found a most unique and attractive substitute for the ordinary Birthday or Christmas Card", stating craftily that "many popular books of this character published in the early part of the century (the 19th) are now worth their weight in gold."

The first title published was **Victoria, the Good Queen and Empress** with 14 illustrations after photographs and paintings, comprising 96 pages. The volume is written by Eleanor Bulley but came out anonymously in the first edition of 1897 and was re-published in an enlarged fourth edition of 110 pages in 1901, including an account of the death of the Queen. It is dedicated "to children in all places of Her Majesty's Dominions". Other royal texts, also written by Eleanor Bulley, are **Life of Edward VII, King of Great Britain and Ireland, and Emperor of India** with 149 pages and 16 illustrations, dated 1901, and **Life of Queen Alexandra,** 185 pages, published in 1902.

THE BOOK OF NOUNS, or Things which may be Seen. London, Darton and Harvey, 1806.

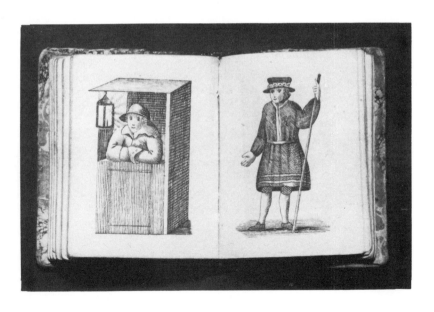

The other titles, all dated 1901, are **The Enchanted Doll** by Mark Lemon, illustrated by Richard Doyle; **The Story without an End** by Friedrich Wilhelm Carové, told in English by Sarah Austin and with illustrations by Aimée G. Clifford, 108 pages; **Favourite Fables for Tiny Tots,** illustrated by A. S. Wilkinson, 151 pages; **Songs of Innocence** by William Blake, with illustrations by Celia Levetus, 118 pages; **The Seven Champions of Christendom** illustrated by the sculptor A. G. Walker, 151 pages, and **The Midget London,** 224 pages and featuring in its illustrations buildings, streets and parks.

This series is very well produced and clearly printed on art paper. With the possible exception of the first title, the volumes are now fairly elusive.

Having described a number of complete children's libraries in miniature we now turn to some of the more important or interesting individual titles published after 1800 in the English language.

One of the most delightful early volumes is **The Book of Nouns, or Things which may be Seen,** intended for very young children and illustrated with 62 enchanting engraved plates. It was published for the first time by Darton and Harvey in 1800 (as dated on the title while we find a different date, the 25th March, 1801, mentioned on page 66), has 128 pages and measures $2\frac{1}{4}$ by $1\frac{13}{16}$ inches. The Spielmann and Houghton copies are both dated 1806.

The same publishers were responsible for **People of all Nations. A Useful Toy for Girl or Boy,** first issued in London in 1800 and reprinted in 1804, 1806 and 1813. It has 64 leaves and measures $2\frac{5}{16}$ by $1\frac{13}{16}$ inches. The contents include a fine picture alphabet of national costume and many other pleasing costume plates. Houghton No. 263 lists an American edition, published in Philadelphia by Jacob Johnson in 1802, printed by Charles and Scott and measuring $2\frac{3}{8}$ by 2 inches.

John Gregory's **A Father's Legacy to his Daughters** is of seminal importance as a work of general education and can be compared in that respect to Mrs. Chapone's **Letters on the Improvement of the Mind.** It was produced by Oliver & Boyd of Edinburgh in a fine miniature edition of 72 pages in about 1805, printed in a very small type and measures $2\frac{5}{8}$ by $1\frac{3}{4}$ inches. The engraved frontispiece shows two little girls kneeling at the bedside of an elderly man wearing a nightcap. Another undated edition by the same publishers has 90 pages. Spielmann, no. 180, lists an earlier edition, printed by J. Robertson in Edinburgh in 1793, measuring $2\frac{7}{8}$ by $1\frac{3}{4}$ inches, of 88 pages.

Of the many other English-language miniature books for children we can only single out a few. **Peep at the Fair,** printed by T. Brandard in Birmingham circa 1810 is one of the small number of chapbooks which come in their size near to the miniature format, measuring $3\frac{1}{8}$ by $2\frac{1}{4}$ inches. It has 26 charming woodcuts showing circus scenes, including a juggler, a lion, Punch and Judy, etc.

PEOPLE OF ALL NATIONS. Philadelphia, 1802.

Very popular appears to have been a pious work by the Rev. James Janeway with the rather sickening title **A Token for Children: Being an Account of the Conversion, Holy Lives and Joyful Deaths of several young Children,** in two parts. It was published and sold around the year 1840 at Christie's Bible-Warehouse in London, has an engraved frontispiece and two title pages, size $2\frac{1}{8}$ by $1\frac{1}{4}$ inches. This well-printed volume of 208 pages was issued in publishers' gilt-tooled morocco with gilt edges and is dedicated to "all parents, school-masters and school-mistresses". A much more appropriate juvenile item is the tiny and very rare **The Golden Alphabet, or Parents' Guide and Child's Instructor** with woodcut alphabet headings. It was published, presumably in London, in 1846 by Robert Taylor, bound in red wrappers and has 126 pages, size $\frac{3}{4}$ by $\frac{13}{16}$ of an inch.

Three very pleasing little books, meant chiefly as Christmas presents, were published in 1838 and 1841. The earlier item is **The Fairy Annual,** "edited by Robin Goodfellow, attending sprite to their Majesties Oberon and Titania". It was published by Joseph Robins in London and finely printed by Richard Watts, has VI, 119 pages and measures $1\frac{11}{16}$ by $1\frac{3}{8}$ inches. The pseudonymous author dedicated the volume to Queen Victoria. It contains fairy tales and short stories by various minor authors and was chiefly designed for children. The other two books, both written by Barnard Crecerelle, are **The Lilliputian Forget-Me-Not** and **The Lilliputian Sacred Annual,** both published by Robert Tyas in London in 1841. They each have 124 pages of text and six very finely engraved plates, are clearly and legibly printed in 4 and 5 point type, and measure $1\frac{5}{8}$ by $1\frac{1}{4}$ inches. Charmingly bound in lilac or red watered silk with gilt edges, they must have made most desirable presents for grown-ups and children alike.

Equally delightful is **The Little Forget-Me-Not. A Love Token,** with 12 most attractive engraved plates, which was published by Charles Tilt in London about 1845, measuring $2\frac{5}{8}$ by $2\frac{1}{8}$

71

inches. Bound in gilt-stamped cloth with nicely designed vignettes on both covers, its 176 pages contain poems and short stories.

In about 1880 the London toy firm of W. H. Cremer, Junr. issued a small publicity volume for children entitled **Dolly's Album, arranged for Little Ladies.** It contains 14 small photographs of toys, tiny furniture and of "Dolly's Toy Shop" as well as of "Dolly's Friend", the bearded owner of the European Toy Warehouse at 210 Regent's Street. This miniature curiosity measures $2\frac{1}{8}$ by $1\frac{7}{8}$ inches and is bound in blind-stamped leather contained in a similar slipcase. Amongst the pictures are "Dolly in the Row", showing her on horseback, "Dolly taking an Airing" in a coach drawn by two horses and "Dolly's Exhibition Bedstead".

More common, but much sought after, is Kate Greenaway's **Alphabet** with coloured illustrations including decorated initials for each letter of the A.B.C. showing small children at play. It was published by George Routledge in London in the 1880's, bound in coloured pictorial glazed boards measuring $2\frac{11}{16}$ by $2\frac{3}{8}$ inches.

Messrs. Bryce in Glasgow, the assiduous and successful publishers of miniature books to whom we are devoting a special chapter, issued a very attractive tiny book specifically intended for children. It is **My Tiny Alphabet Book** comprising "Tiny Alphabet of Animals" and "Tiny Alphabet of Birds", two parts in one volume. It is undated but was published around the year 1900 and measures $1\frac{1}{2}$ by $1\frac{1}{8}$ inches. In its gilt-stamped red leather binding it contains two complete alphabets printed in colour. Quite frequently the lower covers were used to advertise Mellins Food, while other copies show a horse and a bird in flight on both covers.

At about the same time, A. Treherne in London published a small volume entitled **Baby's Own Book** with coloured illustrations by R. Coutts Armour. It depicts boldly various familiar animals including a pigeon, a goat, a cat, a cow, a hen and even a rat, is bound in pictorial boards and printed on thick art paper on one side of the leaf only and measures $1\frac{13}{16}$ by $1\frac{1}{16}$ inches. Because of the nature of its binding, very few copies have survived intact the eager attentions of their baby readers. A similar volume issued by Treherne **Baby's ABC** is mentioned in *The Miniature Book Collector,* Volume II, No. 2, containing the familiar "A was an Apple Pie", etc. on 44 leaves. It was printed by the Graphis Colour Printing Works.

In 1912 or thereabouts Henry Frowde and Hodder & Stoughton in London published a number of small children's books, measuring $2\frac{5}{8}$ by $2\frac{3}{8}$ inches, bound in pictorial boards of which we would especially like to mention **Little Pink Petticoat, Scrappety Hop and Pearly Top,** both with coloured frontispieces, **Puss in the Palace, The little Old Woman of X** and **The Ugly Princess.** Quite a few other titles were issued in this series, published under the auspices of the Oxford University Press.

During the 19th century many miniature children's books in the English language made their appearance in the United States of America. Very popular were the books written by Frances Elizabeth Barrow (1822-1894) under the pen-name of "Aunt Laura". We have seen **Grandma's Story of the vain little Girl, The Bunch of Grapes, Bird Stories** and **Carl's Visit to the Child Island,** all published by Breed, Butler & Co. in Buffalo in 1863. Other titles are **The Silver Medal, Little Comfort, Morsels of History, Fanny's Journey** and **The Dolls' Surprise Party,** all published during the same year and varying in size from 2 by $1\frac{1}{2}$ to $1\frac{3}{8}$ by $\frac{15}{16}$ inches.

A series of six American children's books was published by S. R. Urbino in Boston, Mass. in 1864, comprising 55 to 69 pages, measuring $2\frac{5}{16}$ by $1\frac{9}{16}$ inches and bound in olive cloth. The titles are **The Lost Baby, Willie's Vacation** in two volumes, **Dick Lee: A Fairy Story in Short Easy Words, Downy and her Kittens** and **Little Chimney Sweeper.**

In 1896 a **Little Folks Library** was published

by the Werner Company of Chicago and New York. Amongst the titles are **Circus Day** by George Ade, **Stones from History** by John Hazelden and **Little Farmers** by W. O. Krohn. The volumes comprise 125 to 127 pages, measure $2\frac{3}{8}$ by $2\frac{1}{8}$ inches and are bound in red or blue boards.

A FATHER'S LEGACY TO HIS DAUGHTERS, by Dr. Gregory. Edinburgh, ca. 1810. Contemporary red morocco binding.

CHAPTER TEN

FOREIGN CHILDREN'S BOOKS AFTER 1800

The French were particularly successful in publishing beautifully illustrated and finely produced children's books in small format. In their best examples they combine superb printing, exquisitely designed illustrations and imaginative and original bindings with very attractive texts.

A "Bibliothèque en Miniature pour la Jeunesse" was published around 1820 by Gide Fils of Paris, measuring $2\frac{5}{8}$ by $2\frac{1}{2}$ inches. The titles comprise **La Botanique, Histoire des Oiseaux, Histoire de France, Contes Arabes, Contes Moraux, Histoire des Insectes,** and **Histoire des Quadrupèdes,** each with 4 engraved plates with the exception of the **Contes Arabes** which has only 3 plates. All the illustrations are coloured by hand. The volumes are usually bound in red boards and stored in a special glass-topped box.

Another "Bibliothèque en Miniature" bears that collective title only on the spine of the slipcase which houses the six enticing volumes belonging to this set for young people. It was published by the Paris firm of Marcilly who were responsible for many of the most beautiful children's books of the period. The set includes Berquin's Variétés, Demoustier's Mythologie, Florian's Mélanges, La Fontaine's Fables and Poésies by Millevoye and by Voltaire. Each volume has 24 pages printed in a very small type by Firmin Didot Frères, half of them are bound in pink and the other half in green wrappers and they measure $2\frac{3}{4}$ by $1\frac{13}{16}$ inches. The slipcase is shaped like a book, has a finely gilt-tooled leather spine and measures 3 by $2\frac{1}{16}$ inches.

In 1823 Augustin Legrand of Paris brought out a "Petite Bibliothèque Portative" in 10 volumes, in printed wrappers and preserved in their original case. Like so many contemporary children's books, the titles combine instruction with amusement. They are **Morale en Action, Mythologie, Geographie Universelle** with a folding map, **Fables, Histoire de France, Contes, Animaux, Insectes et Oiseaux, Minéralogie et Poissons** and **Botanique,** all illustrated with pleasant engraved plates and measuring $2\frac{9}{16}$ by $2\frac{7}{16}$ inches.

Spielmann No. 291a lists a set with the imprint "Imprimerie de Rignoux", bound in pink boards and preserved in its original glass-topped box.

We can only mention a few characteristic examples of the large number of splendid French children's books in miniature size published during the first half of the 19th century. The following were all published by Marcilly in Paris and are undated: **Les Petites Histoires,** 4 volumes each with a fine coloured engraved frontispiece and containing stories like "Le Turc bienfaisant", "La Poupée", "Le Loup des Champs" and "Le Chien de Liverpool". Their size is $2\frac{3}{4}$ by $1\frac{7}{8}$ inches — **Petite Galerie Mythologique** contains a folding strip with 24 engravings representing gods of the ancient world and measures $2\frac{7}{16}$ by $1\frac{13}{16}$ inches — **La Petite Corbeille des Fleurs** is a lovely volume with fine hand-coloured title vignette and 8 beautiful coloured engravings of flowers. It is bound in richly and finely gilt-tooled calf and measures $2\frac{1}{4}$ by $1\frac{5}{8}$ inches — **Petite Galerie d'Histoire Naturelle** is a 4-volume set, each volume with 2 finely coloured plates and dealing with birds, butterflies, flowers and fruit respectively, the size being a fairly large $3\frac{1}{4}$ by $2\frac{1}{8}$ inches. The books are bound in blind-stamped pink, green, violet and fawn boards and preserved in a pink cardboard slipcase. **Le Petit Conteur d'Anecdotes** has a charming engraved title and 6 ravishing engraved plates, 95 pages, size an oblong $1\frac{5}{8}$ by $2\frac{1}{8}$ inches, is bound in pink boards and excellently printed by A. Firmin-Didot in small type — **Les Cris de Paris,** with lithographed calligraphic title and 27 finely executed coloured lithographed cards illustrating Paris street vendors, is preserved in a cardboard case which in turn fits into a slipcase, measuring $1\frac{5}{8}$ by $1\frac{3}{16}$ inches — **Petite Histoire Grotesque de Pierrot Goulu** published ca. 1835 is a very charming harlequinade of 2 leaves and 124 pages, with 7 exceptionally lively and amusing engraved colour plates. It measures an oblong $2\frac{1}{8}$ by $2\frac{7}{8}$ inches. Another oblong volume, **Le Petit La Fontaine** came out in several Marcilly editions and measures in at least one of them $1\frac{7}{8}$ by $2\frac{3}{8}$ inches. It has six fine coloured illustrations of fables (**Mikrobiblion,** no. 141, Spielmann, no. 290).

Other children's miniatures published by Marcilly between 1820 and 1830 are **Enfantines** with engraved title and 6 ravishing plates, $2\frac{1}{8}$ by $1\frac{9}{16}$, inches, bound in ivory-covered boards, 92 pages finely printed by Firmin Didot in tiny type; **Contes à mes Petits Amis,** with engraved pictorial title and 6 plates, 94 pages, oblong $1\frac{5}{8}$ by $2\frac{3}{16}$ inches; **L'Education de la Poupée** with engraved title and 7 endearing plates describing the life of a doll, bound in pink blind-stamped boards in similar slipcase, 126 pages, oblong $2\frac{1}{4}$ by $2\frac{15}{16}$ inches; **Petite Excursion en France** with engraved pictorial title and 11 fine plates illustrating French provincial costume, bound in lilac boards in similar slipcase, 128 pages, 3 by $2\frac{1}{8}$ inches, the text being a description of the French regions.

Of smaller size and found perhaps more frequently than the above-mentioned books are the many editions of **Petit Fabuliste** or **Petit Fabuliste de la Jeunesse,** each with 6 engraved or woodcut plates, printed in the earlier editions by Firmin Didot and later by Presteau in Paris, with bindings varying from ivory sides with velvet spine to red or green gilt morocco, and in some cases boards with lithographed borders or even simple blue wrappers. The size most commonly found is $1\frac{1}{4}$ by 1 inch but we have seen much larger editions published by Marcilly and printed by A. Pinard, measuring 3 by $2\frac{1}{8}$ inches. None of the issues is dated but they all came out between 1820 and 1850.

Two religious children's books of very small size must have been published in large numbers over quite a long period. They are **Le Petit Paroissien de l'Enfance** and **Le Petit Paroissien de la Jeunesse** which often bear the Marcilly imprint and were printed by Firmin Didot, Ad. B. Lainé, Rignoux, René et Cie., Maulde-Renou, Langlumé et Peltier, Eberhart and others in Paris and L. Lefort in Lille, Martial Ardant in Limoges and perhaps in other towns as well. These attractive prayerbooks for children measure usually about $1\frac{1}{8}$ by $\frac{13}{16}$ inches, have engraved titles and 5 plates, varying a great deal in quality and even design. Some of the illustrations are engraved in wood. Spielmann, nos. 403 and 404 and **Mikrobiblion,** nos. 175 to 182 list some of these editions. We have seen them in all kinds of bindings, in red morocco gilt, in ivory covers with velvet spine, in stiff gilt wrappers, in green or red boards, some with the calligraphic inscription "Messe" on the front-cover. A late edition was attractively bound in pinchbeck covers with the image of the Virgin Mary on the front-cover and a cross on the lower cover, blue cloth spine and a clasp. Although not rare these titles are much collected because of their small size and pleasing illustrations. As there exist so many variants it is possible to bring together quite a large collection consisting only of these tiny devotional books.

During the last few years of the nineteenth century, Pairault in Paris published two remarkable series of children's books. The first comprises 10 volumes, all dated 1896 and measuring $1\frac{3}{4}$ by $1\frac{1}{4}$ inches. They are printed on fairly indifferent paper and the type used appears to be 8-point. Each volume is bound in stiff wrappers of different colours, with the title lithographed in gilt on front-cover and spine. The texts are very clearly directed towards children and consist mainly of fairy tales and fables. They are **Aladdin ou La Lampe Merveilleuse, Conte tiré des Mille et Une Nuits,** 57 pages — **Ali Baba ou les Quarante Voleurs,** 58 pages — **L'Enfant Prodigue. Le Juif Errant,** 60 pages — **Fénelon: Fables et Allégories,** 61 pages — **La Fontaine: Quelques Fables,** 59 pages — **Florian: Quelques Fables,** 61 pages — **Hégésippe Moreau: Le Neveu de la Fruitière (Lazare Hoche),** 64 pages — **Perrault: Le Petit Chaperon Rouge. Les Fées. Contes,** 60 pages — **Chanoine Schmid: Quelques Contes,** 60 pages — **Morel de Vinde: La Morale de l'Enfance,** 62 pages.

Miniature books published by Pairault in Paris, 1895-98, in their original bookcase, "La Gracieuse".

These ten volumes can be housed in a very elegant miniature bookcase specially created by the publishers. Called "La Gracieuse" it is covered by patterned damask decorated with gold thread and has a glazed door and glass shelf. It measures $5\frac{1}{4}$ by $3\frac{9}{16}$ inches, and is meant to imitate the Louis XV style.

The same splendid case also serves to house the second Pairault miniature set, which is much better produced and has very interesting illustrations. It is smaller, measuring $1\frac{1}{2}$ by $1\frac{3}{16}$ inches, and the print is $5\frac{1}{2}$-point and much neater. The stiff wrappers of the bindings are again in different colours and the front-wrappers bear a reproduction of the title pages. The volumes were issued in different degrees of luxuriousness, the cheapest at a cost of 1.50 francs, being on "papier velin" in paper wrappers. The same issue bound in morocco was priced at 3 francs, while copies on Japanese vellum cost 5 francs when printed in black, and 6 francs when printed in red. The copies printed "sur Japon" were numbered and limited to 50 in each of the two print colours and they have each two sets of illustrations.

The titles are: **Le Petit Poucet** by Charles Perrault with four illustrations by the famous Steinlen, 1895, 60 pages — **Les Rondes de l'Enfance** with fine illustrations by Steinlen, 1895, 78 pages including musical notation for the children's songs — **Jeanne d'Arc** by H. Buffenoir with four illustrations by G. Maire, 1895, 98 pages — **La Souris Blanche** by Hégésippe Moreau with four illustrations by Henri Pille, 1895, 104 pages — **Jeannot et Colin** by Voltaire with five illustrations by Steinlen, 1895, 85 pages, followed by **Le Minuscule. Revue Mensuelle, Octobre 1895,** a miniature periodical of 16 pages advertising and illustrating the above-mentioned bookcase "La Gracieuse" and generally considered the smallest original miniature periodical in existence — **Fortunée** by Madame d'Aulnoy with four illustrations by F. Régamey, 1896, 84 pages, followed by five pages advertising the volumes in this "Collection

Minuscule" — **La Filleule du Seigneur. Histoire du Chien de Brisquet** by Charles Nodier with five illustrations by M. Moisand, 1897, 66 pages and five pages of advertisements — **Boum-Boum** by Jules Claretie with five illustrations by Ch. Jouas, 1898, 64 pages.

This beautifully illustrated set is particularly interesting because of the bibliophile ploy used by the publishers to print in addition to the ordinary copies a strictly limited and numbered edition on superior paper in what Pairault calls a "tirage de luxe".

El Diamantino Librito de Misa de los Niños, (The little diamond Book of the Mass for children), was specially dedicated to Latin American children and published around 1850 by the firm of La Place Sanchez & Cia. in Paris. This Spanish text was attractively bound in mother-of-pearl covers with brass clasp and velvet spine and measures $2\frac{1}{4}$ by $1\frac{5}{8}$ inches.

We mention only one German miniature book for children. Its title is **Puppen-Lieder,** (Songs for Dolls), with 14 illustrations and was published by B. Roges in Frankfurt-am-Main circa 1860, measuring $1\frac{5}{8}$ by $1\frac{3}{16}$ inches. The illustrations are lithographed and the little volume is printed by Klimsch & Co. (see **Mikrobiblion,** no. 207). Although very rich in juvenilia of great quality, 19th century Germany appears to have been more addicted to much larger volumes, of quarto and even folio size, but many octavo and even duodecimo editions can be found. Some beautifully

LA FILLEULE DU SEIGNEUR, by Charles Nodier, Paris, Pairault & Cie, 1897. Title page.

illustrated colour plate books for children were printed in Guben, Silesia but although they are of very small size and make their appearance in miniature book sales, they exceed the 3-inch limit.

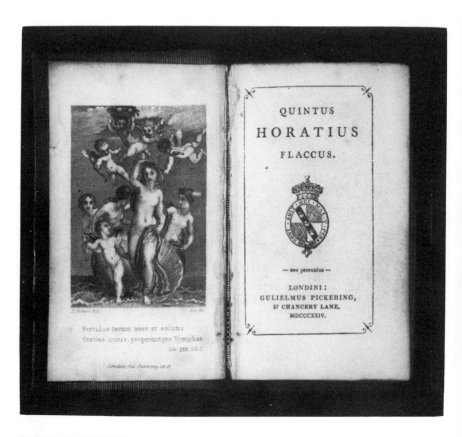

POEMS OF QUINTUS
HORATIUS FLACCUS.
London, Pickering, 1824.
Frontispiece and title page.

CHAPTER ELEVEN

TRAVELLING LIBRARIES AND PICKERING'S DIAMOND CLASSICS

Many of the great milestones of human achievement in the fields of literature and philosophy have served to inspire the makers of miniature books, and resulted in some of their finest creations. During the hundred or so years preceding World War I, the reading habit had been acquired by social strata who before the French, and even more before the industrial revolution never touched a book. The rapid expansion of coach, and later railway services, gave additional impetus to the sale of small eminently portable books and led to the creation of special travelling libraries.

Although the height of all the volumes contained in them exceeds the three-inch limit, we do not for a moment hesitate about including them in this book, especially two libraries, one in English and one in French, expressly created for travellers. We are also including in this chapter the famous series of "Diamond Classics" published by Messrs. Pickering of London. Their miniature character is unmistakable, they are printed in small or even tiny type and their entire conception is firmly based on the principle of miniaturisation.

The earliest of travelling libraries is the "Bibliothèque Portative du Voyageur", published and printed by J. B. Fournier Père et Fils in Paris in 1802. Each volume measures $3\frac{5}{8}$ by $2\frac{11}{16}$ inches and its 49 tomes are housed in a leather-covered box which is lockable and has, when closed, the appearance of a large folio-sized book. A list of the contents is pasted to the inside of the case so that its completeness can be checked. The library comprises the plays of Corneille in five, those of Racine in four and the theatrical works of Voltaire in five volumes. The Molière has seven volumes. There are also the works of Boileau, Gresset, Pierre de Bernis, Vergier and Grécourt and Voltaire's **La Pucelle d'Orléans** each in one volume, while Piron and La Fontaine's **Fables and Contes** are each contained in two volumes. Many volumes have portraits of their authors. The prose works include Montesquieu's **Grandeur des Romains,** Bossuet's **Discours sur l'Histoire Universelle** in

3 volumes, the **Histoire de Gil Blas** by Lesage in five volumes, Demoustier's **Lettres à Émilie** in three volumes, while the splendid memoirs of Philibert de Gramont have two volumes. The following are complete in one volume each: The famous **Les Amours de Daphnis et Chloé,** the less well known **Histoire du Petit Jehan de Saintre et de Gérard de Nevers,** finally the **Voyages de Télémaque** by Fénelon. This remarkable library in miniature thus includes many of the most prodigious and important works in the French language, but instead of requiring a very large bookcase it is contained in just one very portable case. It is frequently assumed that it was this travelling library which Napoleon Bonaparte carried with him during his campaigns. Spielmann, No. 49, lists only the Montesquieu and adds "The miniature format serves here a definite and acknowledged purpose". Complete sets are of the utmost rarity and I have only seen one nearly complete set, which now occupies pride of place in the library of an American collector.

A most impressive and splendid English travelling library was published by Jones & Co. at the Temple of the Muses in Finsbury Square, London. It consists of the "Diamond Poets" and the "Diamond Classics" which were printed in the tiny diamond type over a period of eight years between 1824 and 1832. Each volume has a finely designed engraved frontispiece and title, followed by a printed title and is bound very attractively in pink or dark-green corded silk with gilt edges. The size of each volume is $3\frac{3}{4}$ by $2\frac{1}{4}$ inches. The edition is housed in a wooden bookcase covered with maroon morocco and consists of two hinged wings each with two shelves and lined with pink paper. When fully opened they form a beautiful large case the top of which resembles a classical temple and is lettered "Jones Diamond Poets & Classics". When closed the case protects completely the leather-hinged glass doors and the books behind them. It then resembles two quarto-sized books and can be locked with a key. In its extended form it measures 9 by 17 inches.

Each case has a printed label stuck to the inside which gives the contents of the 53 volumes. That list is preceded by the following advertising paeon of praise: "A curious miniature edition (the smallest ever printed), combining the advantages of portability with clear and beautiful printing, embellished with fine portraits of the authors, and vignette titles, at the undermentioned prices in silk binding with gilt leaves: or the whole complete in a case the size of one quarto volume, at very trifling additional expense, forming a Portable Travelling Library".

The label lists the following titles and prices; in the shillings and pence currency of the time:

Akenside's Pleasures of Imagination, &c. 3s. 6d; Beattie's Minstrel and other Poems, 1s. 6d; Butler's Hudibras, 4s. 0d; Burn's Poems, 2 vols., 6s. 6d; Byron's Select Works, 3s. 6d; Bloomfield's Farmer's Boy, 1s. 6d; Canning's Poems, 2s. 0d; Cowper's Poems, 2 vols., 6s. 0d; Collin's Poetical Works, 2s. 0d; Dryden's Poetical Works, 2 vols., 8s. 0d; Dryden's Virgil, 5s. 0d; Dodd's Beauties of Shakespeare, 3s. 6d; Falconer's Shipwreck, &c., 2s. 0d; Gifford's Baviad and Maeviad, 3s. 0d; Goldsmith's Poems, 2s. 0d; Gray's Poetical Works, 2s. 0d; Grahame and Logan's Poems, 3s. 6d; Gay's Fables, &c., 3s. 6d; Hayley's Triumphs of Temper, 2s. 0d; Lyttleton & Hammond, 2s. 6d; Milton's Paradise Lost, 3s. 6d; Milton's Paradise Regained, 3s. 6d; Mason's English Garden, 2s. 0d; More's Sacred Dramas, &c., 3s. 6d; Pope's Poetical Works, 2 vols., 7s. 6d; Prior's ditto, 2 vols., 6s. 6d; Richardson's (D.L.) Sonnets, &c., 3s. 6d; Somerville's Chase, &c., 2s. 0d; Shenstone's Poems, 3s. 6d; Smith's (Charlotte) Sonnets, 2s. 0d; Thomson's Seasons, 2s. 6d; Watt's Lyrics, &c., 3s. 6d; White's (Kirke) Remains, 2 vols., 6s. 6d; Young's Night Thoughts, &c., 4s. 0d; Crabbe's Village and other Poems, 2s. 0d.

These "Diamond Poets" are followed by the

"Diamond Classics", a Prose Series, uniform with the above:

Bacon's Essays, 3s. 6d; Castle of Otranto, 2s. 0d; Elizabeth, or the Exiles of Siberia, 2s. 0d; Gulliver's Travels, 5s. 0d; Goldsmith's Vicar of Wakefield, 3s. 0d; Leland's Demosthenes, 2 vols., 7s. 6d; Paul and Virginia, 3s. 0d; Rasselas (Dr. Johnson), 2s. 6d; Sterne's Journey, 2s. 6d; Sorrows of Werther (Goethe), 2s. 6d; Theodosius and Constantia, 3s. 0d.

As can be seen from this extensive list, the 53 volumes cover a large field of English literature, combining great and famous works with some now almost forgotten texts. Spielmann, nos. 229 to 275, lists most of these titles. In his comments on travelling libraries he mentions that assembled by Sir Julius Caesar which did not include miniature books, was assembled in the early 17th century, and is now in the British Library.

Although not assembled in a specially created travelling case, "Pickering's Diamond Classics" published in London and comprising English, Greek, Latin and Italian classics, serve a very similar purpose. Due to the great editorial care and the superb printing and binding which went into their manufacture, combined with the importance of their contents, these little volumes are now very eagerly collected by many minibibliophiles, and even more generally by lovers of finely produced books. All of them exceed however the 3-inch limit.

The first book published by William Pickering in miniature size is the **Quintus Horatius Flaccus** issued in 1820 and printed like many other small books in this series by C. Corrall in a fine and most legible diamond type, $4\frac{1}{2}$-point. It has a portrait engraved by R. Grave and the engraved title bears a vignette showing a lyre within a wreath. It is followed by a printed title. At the end of the 185 pages there are 3 unnumbered pages followed in some copies by the rare "corrigenda" slip. Although frequently found in very attractive contemporary or later morocco bindings, Pickering issued his miniature editions in cloth with printed paper labels on the spines and the Horace is reputed to be the first English book issued in publisher's cloth. The volume measures $3\frac{5}{16}$ by 2 inches. Pickering issued a second edition of the Horace in 1824, the size being $3\frac{1}{2}$ by $2\frac{1}{4}$ inches. It has an engraved frontispiece designed by Stothard.

Brunet III, 323 calls the Horace a "jolie petite édition", and points out that there exist copies printed on china paper as well as six copies printed on vellum. These latter rarities bear the manuscript inscription signed by William Pickering: "Six copies only of this edition have been printed upon vellum". The size of these vellum copies is $3\frac{1}{4}$ by $2\frac{1}{16}$ inches. The only other titles which were issued on vellum are the Virgil of 1821, the Cicero of the same year, the Terence of 1822 and the Catullus, Tibullus and Propertius of 1824. It seems strange that Pickering produced also large-paper copies with very wide margins of some of his miniature classics and especially the 1824 Horace is not infrequently found in such a much larger format. However it seems to us rather incongruous to make every effort to produce fine volumes in a very compact edition and in tiny print and then enlarge the size by issuing such large-paper copies.

The **Publius Virgilius Maro** of 1821 has an engraved portrait by Grave and engraved and printed titles and comprises 283 pages including a dedication leaf to Earl Spencer. It measures $3\frac{3}{8}$ by $1\frac{15}{16}$. According to Sheringham in his article in *The Connoisseur* of November 1902, this is the rarest of the diamond classics as "only a hundred copies survived a fire" at the printers, and he adds that "a complete copy is becoming valuable". However we have seen quite a few of them over the years.

The next title to appear was **Petrarca's Le Rime** in Italian. As always in his foreign language miniature editions, the publisher puts his imprint in the language concerned, here "a spesi di G. Pickering, Londra". The portrait is engraved by R. Grave after a design by R. Morghen. The dedication to Earl Spencer is in Italian. The book has 237 numbered and nine unnumbered pages including a leaf advertising the "miniature classics", the size is $3\frac{5}{8}$ by $2\frac{1}{8}$ inches. During the same year Pickering issued his two-volume edition of **Tasso's Gerusalemme Liberata,** again with portrait by the same artists as the Petrarch. The pagination is continuous up to page 405, followed by 3 pages of advertisements. The size is $3\frac{1}{2}$ by $2\frac{1}{8}$ inches. **Dante's Divina Commedia** followed in 1823, a two-volume set with portrait by the same artists as the other Italian volumes. The continuous pagination up to page 374 is followed by four advertisement pages and the size is $3\frac{5}{8}$ by $2\frac{1}{8}$ inches. It may be of interest to know that the two volumes were sold for 10s. in their original cloth.

There followed two Latin editions, the **Publius Terentius Afer** in 1823 and the **Catullus, Tibullus et Propertius** in 1824. The portrait of Terence is designed by Visconti, the book has 220 pages and measures $3\frac{3}{8}$ by $1\frac{15}{16}$ inches. The Catullus of the same size has a frontispiece engraved by A. Fox after Stothard and comprises 92 pages, followed by 2 pages of advertisements.

The first "diamond classic" in English is the superb 9-volume edition of **Shakespeare's Plays** which was also issued in 38 parts bound in printed wrappers. The parts are dated 1823 while the edition in cloth is dated 1825. The volumes measure $3\frac{3}{8}$ by $1\frac{7}{8}$ inches, the parts and a very small number of the bound sets are splendidly illustrated with 38 plates, most of them designed by Thomas Stothard (1755-1834), a leading illustrator of the period and engraved by H. Adlard, F. S. Engleheart, Augustus Fox, R. Grave, C. Marr, T. White and W. H. Worthington. The latter also contributed the design of two plates, while Sir Joshua Reynolds, H. Howard, R. Westall, T. Kirk, W. Peters and Joseph Wright are the designers of some of the other illustrations. Sheringham writes that "the plates were all lost and the later copies are without them" which explains the comparative rarity of illustrated sets. Not very many of them survive in their original cloth as previous owners valued them so highly that they had them bound in morocco. We once saw a magnificent set in finely gilt-tooled cerise morocco and gilt edges, worthy of the infinite care which had been lavished on this very nearly perfect miniature edition. Brunet V, 341 points out that some sets were printed on china paper and sold for four guineas.

Other editions of English classics followed. In 1825 appeared **The Compleat Angler, or The Contemplative Man's Recreation** by Izaak Walton and Charles Cotton, printed by Thomas White in a slightly larger type and with fine frontispiece and engraved title after Stothard. The book has 318 pages with some woodcut illustrations in the text and measures 4 by $2\frac{7}{16}$ inches. In 1827 there followed Walton's **The Lives of Donne, Wotton, Hooker, Herbert and Sanderson,** also printed by White and decorated with a multi-portrait frontispiece engraved by A. Fox after Stothard, 442 pages, measuring 4 by $2\frac{5}{16}$ inches. Like the previous title it was sold for 6 shillings. The last English author in this series is Milton whose **Paradise Lost** came out in 1828 and was printed in diamond type by D. Sidney. The frontispiece by Fox after Stothard shows Milton composing his masterpiece. The size is even larger than that of the two previously mentioned volumes, $4\frac{1}{16}$ by $2\frac{7}{16}$ inches in its original cloth.

The series ended with two Greek editions. The first is the **Novum Testamentum Graecum** of 1828 with frontispiece of Leonardo da Vinci's Last Supper engraved by Worthington. Printed by Corrall in a very fine and clear Greek type, it is one of the glories of these Pickering editions and has been much praised by the bibliographers. The volume comprises 512 pages followed by 8 advertisement pages and measures $3\frac{3}{8}$ by $1\frac{13}{16}$ inches.

The second title is the splendid Homer comprising the **Ilias,** 351 pages and the **Odyssey,** 272 pages, measuring $3\frac{1}{2}$ by 2 inches, a two-volume set which Pickering brought out in 1831. It was printed by the famous Charles Whittingham, has an unsigned frontispiece portrait and the title page is decorated with Pickering's fine anchor device adapted from Aldus with the inscription "Aldi Discip. Anglus". Spielmann, No. 198 describes the Homer as "one of the best-printed Greek miniature books ever produced, with a clear, easily legible type." Brunet III, 277 writes that this is the most portable edition of Homer and mentions that some copies were printed on large paper, others on china paper and twelve on vellum.

While I was writing this chapter, a collector brought to my notice a very late addition to the series of Pickering miniature volumes which must be of the greatest rarity. It is **Manchester al Mondo.** "A Contemplation of Death and Immortality", written by Henry Mountagu, Earl of Manchester and published in London by Pickering and Co. in 1880. It is printed by C. Whittingham at the Chiswick Press, has LXIV, 260 pages and measures $3\frac{3}{8}$ by $2\frac{1}{4}$ inches. Both in size and character it is closely allied to the miniature classics issued fifty years earlier.

To conclude this chapter I should mention a set of French miniature classics, "Classiques en Miniature" published by Dufour et Compagnie in Paris in 1826 and printed by Jules Didot aîné in a clear diamond size type. We have before us the **Oeuvres** of Racine in 4 volumes with a good engraved portrait frontispiece, measuring $3\frac{11}{16}$ by $2\frac{3}{8}$ inches. In the quality of its paper, printing and general appearance it cannot compare with the Pickering classics which occupy a towering height in the world of miniature books.

CHAPTER TWELVE

MICROSCOPIC TYPE IN NINETEENTH CENTURY MINIATURE BOOKS

After the fully justified excursion into slightly larger formats, we now return to books which fit into our self-imposed height limit of 3 inches and are in addition outstanding examples of characteristically small miniature type.

One of the acknowledged miracles of microscopic printing, and in its quality unparalleled to this day, is the type created in the 1820's by Henri Didot the Elder, using the polyamatype method invented by him. It is only $2\frac{1}{2}$-point while the "Diamond Roman" used by Corrall in the Pickering editions is $4\frac{1}{2}$-point. In spite of its exceedingly small size Didot's type is of great beauty and amazing clarity. Bigmore & Wyman write in their **Bibliography of Printing** I, 177: "This fount was a high achievement of the typefounder's art. The minuteness was such that the types could not be cast in the ordinary way; hence Henri Didot (1765-1852) invented a special apparatus, to which he gave the name of polyamatype, and by means of which they were cast, a hundred letters at a time. These beautiful editions were printed by his brother, Didot jun."

The first volume printed in this type was La Rochefoucauld's **Maximes et Réflexions Morales** published by Lefèvre in Paris in 1827. It has XXVIII and 96 pages and measures $2\frac{5}{8}$ by $1\frac{5}{8}$ inches. All the copies we have seen were magnificently bound in contemporary or later morocco, some signed by famous binders like Trautz-Bauzonnet.

This title was followed in 1828 by the complete works of Horace in Latin, in a text revised by Filon. The **Opera Omnia** of Quintus Horatius Flaccus were published in Paris in identical editions by A. Mesnier and by A. Sautelet. The book has VIII, 229 pages and measures an average of 3 by 2 inches. All the copies I have seen had fine bindings of great beauty in contemporary red or green morocco. A particularly splendid one was bound in delicately gilt-tooled citron morocco signed by the famous binder Capé. Only once did I see a copy of the Mesnier edition bound in contemporary pink boards gilt and with very wide margins, measuring $3\frac{3}{16}$ by 2 inches.

Didot's type was bought in 1850 by the famous Dutch printing firm of Enschedé in Haarlem. They made excellent use of it in their edition of **Evangile de Notre Seigneur Jésus Christ selon Saint Matthieu,** (The Gospel according to St. Matthew) in the version revised by J. F. Ostervald. It was printed by Jean Enschedé et fils in 1900 and measures $2\frac{7}{16}$ by $1\frac{13}{16}$ inches. According to **Mikrobiblion,** no. 90, the clarity and beauty of Didot's type shows up at its best in this masterly edition. While this is a matter of opinion, it is an undisputed fact that this type has survived over a period of seventy years.

A very interesting "feminist" series of very small volumes printed in minute type was published by Marquis in Paris around the year 1820. Each volume measures $1\frac{7}{8}$ by $1\frac{1}{4}$ inches, has 28 pages and contains short extracts from the work of the following prominent ladies: Madame de Lambert, Mademoiselle de L'Espinasse, Madame Necker, Madame de Riccoboni and Madame de Staël. This rare series is attractively bound in decorated flexible boards with gilt edges. Possibly these finely produced volumes were presented to lady purchasers of chocolates.

A distinguished miniature book printed in microscopic type is an edition of La Fontaine's **Fables** issued in what is called an *édition miniature* by the Fonderie Laurent et Deberny in Paris in 1850 with 250 pages, measuring $2\frac{7}{8}$ by $1\frac{15}{16}$ inches. The type is beautifully clear. We have seen an exceptionally fine copy of this distinguished volume in a straight-grained morocco binding signed by David. The same type foundry used the identical tiny type again in 1855 when it brought out Gresset's **Ver-Vert, suivi de la Chartreuse, L'Abbaye et autres Pièces** comprising 163 pages and measuring $2\frac{3}{8}$ by $1\frac{11}{16}$ inches. It was bound in printed wrappers and the publishers called it an *édition mignardise*, a dainty little edition. Kuczynski in his bibliography of the Brockhaus collection, no. 34 describes the type as clear and beautiful. The La Fontaine which was shown as a star exhibit at the 1850 Exhibition, was printed by Plon Frères and the Gresset by Ernest Meyer, both in Paris.

Another work printed in an amazingly small type is Thomas à Kempis's **De Imitatione Christi** published in Paris by Edwin Tross in 1858, using the type of Guiraudet et Jouaust of rue St. Honoré 338 which like the type used for the preceding two volumes is $2\frac{1}{2}$-point. Brunet III, 416 asserts that it is the type cast by Henri Didot. The volume has a wood-engraved frontispiece of Christ, the "Salvator Mundi" and comprises 155 pages. Copies measure approximately $2\frac{3}{4}$ by $1\frac{13}{16}$ inches. This depends on the margins left by the binder of the volume which was issued in printed grey wrappers.

Several other editions of Thomas à Kempis were printed in microscopic type. In our knowledge, the smallest of these volumes is that published by J. Casterman and Sons in Tournai, Belgium, in 1851. It has 509 pages plus the title leaf and measures $2\frac{1}{16}$ by $1\frac{3}{8}$ inches. The type is $4\frac{1}{2}$-point. Although the printing lacks distinction the volume is quite rare.

Of all the microscopically printed miniature books the **Fables** by Ivan Andreievitch Krylof in Russian language is perhaps the most difficult to find. It was published by Jacob de Reiche in St. Petersburg in 1855 and measures $1\frac{3}{16}$ by $\frac{15}{16}$ inches and has 86, (1) pages. It is magnificently printed in an unbelievably small Russian type. The original binding of great delicacy consists of finely lithographed boards using blue and green inks. The publisher was the director of the establishment entrusted with the printing of Russian paper money and the little volume was intended as a specimen. **Mikrobiblion,** No. 137 writes that it counts amongst the greatest rarities and *Nauroy,* page 20 also describes it as *très rare.* The only copy I had the pleasure of handling was that formerly in the Vera von Rosenberg collection.

The most widely discussed and the most sensational of all microscopic type-faces used in minia-

93

ture books is undoubtedly the "fly's eye type", *occhio di mosca* used by the brothers Salmin in Padua for their Dante edition of 1878 and their Galileo of 1896. According to the colophon leaf at the end of the Dante volume the type was made in 1850 by order of Giacomo Gnocchi of Milan who in 1867 asked the brothers Salmin of Padua to use it in an edition of Dante's **Divina Commedia.** Begun at that date, the painfully difficult task proceeded under the supervision of Luigi Busato and was completed eleven years later *a gloria di Dante,* (to the glory of Dante), on the 9th June, 1878 and printed in 1000 copies. The first edition bears the imprint 'Milano, G. Gnocchi edit., Padova, Tip. Salmin, 1878' on the title page and

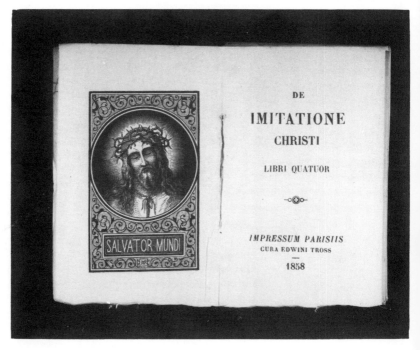

DE IMITATIONE CHRISTI
by Thomas a Kempis. Paris,
Edwin Tross, 1858. Frontispiece
and title page.

94

was issued in printed wrappers. It has 4 leaves, 499 numbered pages followed by the colophon and measures $2\frac{1}{8}$ by $1\frac{3}{8}$ inches. The engraved frontispiece is a portrait of Dante. Ulrico Hoepli, the well-known Milan publisher, bought the leaves during the same year and replaced the title with his own, printed in black and red, with the imprint 'Milano, Ulrico Hoepli, 1878'. Several copies of the *Dantino,* the pet name soon accorded to this edition, can be found in fine morocco bindings; the most beautiful one we have seen was in dark-green crushed morocco with gilt fillets and inside dentelle, a very fine flower tool, in gilt in the centre of both covers and of course with gilt edges.

Many legends have developed around the printing of the Dante and seeing the spindly nature of the minute type it is small wonder that the Grolier Club list, page 129 relates that "the work is said to have seriously injured the eyesight of both the compositor and the corrector. It took one month to print 30 pages and new types were necessary for every new form".

In 1880 Hoepli brought out a companion volume entitled **Galleria Dantesca Microscopica,** a picture book containing 30 tiny photographs reproducing the Dante illustrations by Scaramuzza with accompanying text by C. Fenini. The photographs are of excellent quality and represent perhaps the earliest use of photography in a miniature book. The volume measures $2\frac{3}{16}$ by $1\frac{11}{16}$ inches and the few copies we have been able to see were bound in publisher's citron morocco with finely gilt-tooled covers, and an ornamental centre design on oval maroon leather onlays, raised bands, gilt edges, inside dentelle and endpapers decorated in silver and gold.

The only other book printed by the Salmin brothers in the fly's eye type is **Galileo a Madama Cristina di Lorena (1615)** with a portrait frontispiece and the imprint: Padova, Tipogr. Salmin, 1896. The colophon at the end states: *Stampate coi caratteri del Dantino, Maggio 1897.* The discrepancy between the date on the title and that at the end of the the book indicates that the production of the volume must have overrun its original target date. The volume has 206 pages and measures $\frac{3}{4}$ by $\frac{1}{2}$ of an inch, 18 by 13 mm. For many years this tiny book which is only half the size of an ordinary postage stamp was considered the smallest printed from movable type. I have seen quite a few copies of it over the years, bound either in its original light-blue printed wrappers, in original gilt-stamped vellum, or finely handbound by prominent binders in richly gilt-tooled morocco, inside dentelle and with all edges gilt. It is however surprising that even now very occasionally the book can be found in its original sheets, 64 pages to the sheet, each measuring $13\frac{1}{2}$ by 12 cm., ca. $5\frac{1}{2}$ by $4\frac{3}{4}$ inches. The explanation for such an exceptional survival could be that many binders must have shied away from the fiddling task of making up such a minute volume.

In the *Newsletter of the LXIVmos,* No. 5, page 3 the librarian of Worcester, Mass. Free Public Library writes: "Rarely may it be expected that bibliographical rarity and intense human interest will be combined in one book, yet in the previous little 'Galileo a Cristina di Lorena' is this eminently the case. In this letter to his friend and patron, the great scientist puts forth one of the earliest and most eloquent pleas for the harmony of religion and science."

Another microscopically printed book is the beautiful edition of Petrarca's **Le Rime** in 2 volumes published by Ferd. Ongania in Venice in 1879 in a limited edition of 1000 numbered sets. The book has 354 and 231 pages, the pagination of volume 2 jumping from page 7 to page 16 to allow for the insertion of the *sei sonetti di Francesco Petrarca scoperti e publicati da G. Veludo.* Veludo to whom the publisher dedicates this edition, was the Prefect of the Royal Marciana Library and the six sonnets recently discovered by him are issued here with a separate title. With the exception of that additional text, the book is a reprint of Zatta's Petrarch edition of 1784. The volumes measure $2\frac{3}{4}$

by $2\frac{3}{16}$ inches. Each has a frontispiece portrait of excellent quality and attractive vignettes in the text. In his brief introductory note Ongania explains that he has been encouraged to publish this edition by the success of Salmin's *Dantino* of 1878. It can be assumed that he was much less successful in selling his volumes than Salmin as this Petrarca is exceedingly rare. The Houghton copy, catalogued in the December 1979 sale under No. 270, is beautifully bound in gilt-tooled orange morocco, uncut, with onlaid blue leather borders. The edition is listed in **Mikrobiblion,** No. 189, **Kuczynski,** No. 68, **Tissandier,** page 3 and **Nauroy,** page 77.

Two important miniature books were published in Paris by C. Marpon & F. Flammarion around the year 1880. They are La Fontaine's **Fables** in 2 volumes, 176 and 248 pages, and Silvio Pellico's famous work, **Mes Prisons,** delightfully illustrated by Tony Johannot and comprising 205 pages. Both texts measure $2\frac{3}{16}$ by $2\frac{1}{8}$ inches and are remarkable early examples of a really excellent process of photographic reduction. They are at the same time very successful attempts at the miniaturisation of existing editions of important texts and are usually found in fine morocco or half morocco bindings of the period.

One of the most compendious one-volume works ever published in miniature format is the 1902 edition of Alessandro Manzoni's great novel **I Promessi Sposi.** It is based on the last edition corrected by the Author and has a preface by Fernando Galanti. The printer-publishers are the brothers Salmin of Padua who were responsible for the sensational *Dantino* and the tiny Galileo. In this volume dedicated to Queen Margherita of Savoy they have departed from the use of the ultra-small type used in these earlier volumes and employ a good legible $4\frac{1}{2}$-point type. The volume consists of XV and 1097 numbered pages followed by four unnumbered ones and measures $2\frac{9}{16}$ by $1\frac{3}{4}$ inches. All the copies we have seen were beautifully bound in gilt-stamped calf with finely decorated sides and spine. Spielmann No. 355A writes: "One of the most important and extensive works ever produced in such tiny compass." In an interesting postscript to the Manzoni the publishers discuss the value of miniature books and give some details of their own earlier productions in that field.

When inspecting the miniature book collection of the British Library, I discovered a set of Spanish miniature volumes of high quality and great literary interest I had never encountered before and of which I cannot find any mention in my reference books. They were printed by Miguel Ginesta in Madrid in the 1870's in a fine $4\frac{1}{2}$-point type, measure $3\frac{1}{4}$ by $2\frac{3}{16}$ inches (thus slightly exceeding our 3-inch limit) and are beautifully bound in contemporary richly gilt-stamped Spanish mottled calf. They have a very distinct miniature character. The six volumes are: **Poesias selectas de Fr. Luis de Leon,** 1873 of 77 pages; **Poesias** of Quevedo, 1873, Calderon de la Barca, 1874, Lope de Vega, 1874, Moratin Padre e Hijo, 1874, while the poems of Garcilaso de la Vega and of F. de Rioja appeared in 1875. All these volumes have 96 pages.

A facsimile of the first edition of Goethe's **Die Leiden des jungen Werthers** was published by Adolf Ackermann in Munich in 1880, 224 pages bound in cloth embossed in red with red edges and measuring $2\frac{3}{8}$ by $1\frac{5}{8}$ inches. It was printed *in der Werkstatt der Heinzelmännchen,* (in the workshop of the elves), and constitutes an early reproduction of high quality by photo-zincography.

Edited and printed by Theodore L. de Vinne, the great American printer, a small volume **Brilliants, a setting of Humorous Poetry in Brilliant Type** made its appearance in New York in 1895, comprising XV, 96 pages and measuring $2\frac{1}{4}$ by $1\frac{5}{8}$ inches. In it, the De Vinne Press used the beautiful 4-point brilliant type made by Miller and Richard of Edinburgh. Of particular interest is De Vinne's preface in which he gives a concise and masterly history of miniature typography.

Not infrequently the miniature format attracts some very unusual characters. One of these was Ernest A. Robinson, a printer in Grimsby, who

98

issued in 1891, a tiny volume entitled **The Mite** which remained for many years the smallest English book printed from movable type and may in fact still deserve that distinction. It measures $\frac{3}{4}$ by $\frac{1}{2}$ of an inch, has 30 pages and 8 illustrations. Bound in blue-green wrappers it was "issued as a curiosity" as Robinson states in his introduction. It contains out-of-the-way statistics and printing information. In the reprint of 1896 the printer states on the last leaf "Copy accepted by Her Majesty", in other words Queen Victoria. **The Mite** also forms part of Queen Mary's celebrated Dolls' House Library and is listed on page 381 of E. V. Lucas' account of that library.

Robinson who gives his address on the lower cover of the reprinted edition as being at the Fish Docks opposite the Pontoon in Grimsby, was still going strong in 1930 when he published another curious volume of 8 leaves entitled **Grimsby and Fish,** measuring an oblong $1\frac{7}{8}$ by 2 inches. On the verso of the title page we read: "Authorship, typesetting, printing and published by Ernest A. Robinson, printer and publisher of the Mite, smallest book printed from type". The volume is bound in pale blue wrappers lettered in gilt. The cover gives a new address, 93 Hainton Avenue, much less romantic than the old Fish Docks. The little book contains two poems, one on the history of Grimsby and its fishing industry, the other on fishy by-products. It was printed "on news print made in Grimsby" by Peter Dixon & Sons.

A third tiny volume, dated 1887 and entitled **Sundry Items** was printed and bound by E. A. Robinson together with Parnell & Co. in Grimsby. It has 28 pages and measures $\frac{15}{16}$ by $\frac{3}{4}$ inches. We have seen a copy with an inserted additional leaf on which Robinson states: "200 copies printed by me in 1887. This copy is one of twenty-nine remaining and finished by me in 1931." The book contains like **The Mite** irrelevant and amusing information like for example how many words, letters and verses occur in the bible.

A much more serious and eminently successful

venture was the publication of the **Edizione Vade Mecum** by G. Barbèra in Florence. Printed in tiny but very clear type, that collection of eminent literary works has meant for those addicted to Italian literature, that their beloved books could in the full sense of the word "go with them", as the title of the series indicates. All the volumes measure approximately $2\frac{1}{2}$ by $1\frac{7}{8}$ inches and are beautifully bound in leathers of various colours and lavishly and most attractively gilt-stamped on both sides and spine in ever varying designs. In an interesting preface to the first volume issued in this series, Dante's **Divina Commedia,** dated 1898, the publishers state that they have no intention of producing a microscopic edition but that they aim at creating "the smallest Dante which can be read with the naked eye". The type used was made by the foundry of Flimsch in Frankfurt am Main, and is a $4\frac{1}{2}$-point "Diamant Antiqua". Barbèra's preface ends with a quotation from Th. De Vinne of New York: "In spite of all the protests against their tininess and the damage they can do to the eyesight, miniature books and microscopic type are and will remain great favourites."

The Dante, a volume of 455 pages was also issued in three separate volumes printed on thicker paper than the fine india paper normally used for this text. It is exceedingly rare in that form and has special flowery endpapers designed in green and gold. The Dante proved very popular and we have seen it dated 1899, 1901, 1916, 1922 and even as late as 1935. Another Dante text is **La Vita Nuova e il Canzoniere** issued in 1908. Other texts, all of them produced with great care and immaculate typography, are **Il Tesoretto della Poesia Italiana,** volumes with the **Poesie** of Giacomo Leopardi, Giosuè Carducci, Ugo Foscolo and Giuseppe Giusti, **Le Rime** of Francesco Petrarca, Tasso's **Gerusalemme Liberata,** the **Miranda** by Antonio Fogazzaro, Manzoni's **Liriche Tragedie e Versi Vari,** edited by Giuseppe Lesca, **Patria, Canti Italici da Dante al Carducci, Novelle Poetiche di Vari Autori: Pindemonte, Grossi,**

Sestini, Tommaseo, Prati, Juvenilia by Gabriele d'Annunzio and finally one title in the French language **Livre d'Or de la Poésie Française** which is considered the rarest volume in this "Vade Mecum" series. It comprises VIII, 403 pages and came out in 1900.

A fascinating very small volume is **Konversations-Lexikon** by Daniel Sanders, a miniature encyclopedia in German, published by S. Cohn in Berlin in 1896, reproducing by a photo-lithographic process similar to that used by Bryce in Glasgow, a larger edition published in Berlin by Hugo Steinitz. The book is printed in two columns, comprises 465 pages and measures $\frac{15}{16}$ by $1\frac{1}{4}$ inches, oblong. It is bound in flexible maroon or blue boards, the front-cover stamped in gilt: "Lexikon. Kleinstes Buch der Welt", (Encyclopedia, smallest book in the world). It is preserved in a metal case, has a strong magnifying glass set into the top lid and can be carried on a watch-chain or necklace by means of an attached ring.

It was this very item which introduced me at the age of eleven to the world of miniature books. My

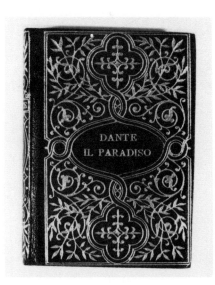

LA DIVINA COMMEDIA, by Dante. Florence, Barbèra, 1898. A volume from the rare edition in three volumes.

father having taken me to the small local bookseller in the suburb where we lived, I spied the volume in a showcase and did not rest until he had bought it for me. Later I relished the secret power of knowledge the minute encyclopedia conferred upon me at the drop of a hat and which made me for a brief but glorious period the envy of my fellow pupils at school.

CHAPTER THIRTEEN

DAVID BRYCE & SONS OF GLASGOW

One of the most prolific and successful makers of miniature books was David Bryce of Glasgow, Scotland, a relatively little known publisher who sallied forth with great vigour and unusually modern marketing methods on making the best of the latest technological advances in the field of photo-lithography. This in no way diminishes his contribution to the printing of tiny books. The exceptional quality of his mechanically reproduced minute creations, the clarity and thus legibility of the texts, shows great mastery in the reduction of larger volumes to the smallest imaginable size by the use of electroplates. In addition, he published some notable works of English literature in slightly larger format although still well within our established size limits. It is no exaggeration if we state that, without his intervention during the closing years of the nineteenth and the first years of the present century, the universe of miniature books would have been much the poorer.

Bryce was greatly helped in his endeavours by the printers of the Glasgow and Oxford University Presses whose reputation for quality and high literary standards must have assisted him not only in the actual production of the books but also in finding the widest possible markets for them, especially in Britain and the United States.

The *Newsletter of the LXIVmos* reprinted in Nos. 11 and 12 an article written by David Bryce which up to then had remained unpublished. In it Bryce who at the time was a retail bookseller describes how he was bitten by the publishing bug as early as in 1876, and then relates his successful ventures into the publication of small and later of minute volumes. He wrote: "Instead of developing works of a larger kind, I descended to the miniature, mite and midget size, producing a little dictionary, the smallest in the world, in a locket accompanied by a magnifying glass. I had many a scoff and jeer as to the absurdity of the production, nevertheless it at once appealed to Mr. Pearson of the notable weekly, who gave me a first order for 3,000 copies and its sales are now over 100,000. Other books

103

followed successfully and latterly a complete Bible. As to the usefulness of such a book one of the commodores of the Castle Packet Lines told me it was the most useful book I had ever published. He constantly carries it in his pocket and reads it with ease with magnifying glass . . .".

Bryce remained in charge of his publishing house until 1913 when he got into financial difficulties and the business was taken over by Gowans & Gray Ltd., with whom he had shared his premises since at least 1911. I may add that Mr. Gowans of that firm was one of my early contacts in the field of minibibliophily.

The earliest miniature books published by Bryce were printed by letterpress and are larger. They include **Bryce's Thumb English Dictionary** with a frontispiece showing a portrait of Dr. Samuel Johnson. That volume measures $2\frac{1}{4}$ by $1\frac{3}{4}$ inches, with 368 numbered pages, most of them of double size, and was issued in various bindings and with different imprints. It came out in the early 1890's and must have been on the market for quite a number of years. We have seen copies with the imprints Glasgow, David Bryce and Son; London, Peacock, Mansfield and Britton; New York, Frederick A. Stokes. They were all printed by the Glasgow University Press. Most of the bindings are in pictorial cloth with an advertisement for Pear's Soap on the lower cover, but a few copies were much more attractively bound in black straight-grained morocco gilt with gold-decorated flowery endpapers and gilt edges or in red roan with red edges gilt.

Amongst these larger miniatures is **Bryce's Thumb Gazeteer of the World,** "comprising the most recent statistical information and notices of the most important historical events associated with the places named, also the last census". It was published by David Bryce in Glasgow in 1893, has VIII, 434 pages (the latter of double size) and measures between $2\frac{1}{8}$ by $1\frac{3}{4}$ and $2\frac{3}{8}$ by $1\frac{7}{8}$ inches. We have seen copies bound in tartan cloth or in red or maroon morocco, all with gilt edges.

104

The Book of Common Prayer was a joint venture with the Oxford University Press who printed the volume. It has 576 pages and measures $2\frac{1}{8}$ by $1\frac{7}{8}$ inches.

Bryce dropped his name from the title of **The Thumb Autograph Book, with Gems of Thought from Classical Authors** which he published circa 1895, measuring $2\frac{5}{16}$ by $1\frac{13}{16}$ inches. Beneath the brief classical quotations the volume provides blank spaces for autographed inscriptions. The publisher states: "The object of this little book is, that with it in your pocket you may get many an autograph not otherwise to be had". We have seen copies with the imprint of Frederick A. Stokes, New York, finely bound in richly and delicately gilt-tooled crimson morocco, with gilt gauffered edges, and copies of the Glasgow edition in black, brown or red morocco, as well as at least one copy in a slipcase and with charming batiqued end-papers.

Another book published with the David Bryce & Son Glasgow imprint in the 1890's is **The Thumb Birthday Text-Book of Short Verses from the Bible** which measures $2\frac{5}{8}$ by $1\frac{3}{4}$ inches and was issued in gilt-tooled morocco, perhaps intended as a birthday present.

The Thumb Confession Book issued for the first time around 1885, measures $2\frac{3}{8}$ by $1\frac{7}{8}$ inches. The little volume has 12 wood-engraved views of Scottish scenery and its pages are gathered in twelve identical sections printed on paper of different tints, including cream, blue, orange and lilac. Each page contains various printed questions of a fairly personal nature with blank pages opposite for the answers. We have seen copies bound in cloth with a gilt-stamped design on the upper cover and red edges while others were in red roan with gilt edges.

Of particular interest is the **Tom Thumb Calendar, Diary, and Proverb Book for 1893** which was printed for David Bryce and Son by the Glasgow University Press and measures $2\frac{1}{8}$ by $1\frac{5}{8}$ inches. It has an introduction dealing with dwarfs in general and the famous "General Tom Thumb" in particular. It has a woodcut frontispiece and the blue cloth binding is pictorially gilt-stamped with a design showing the "General" in his carriage.

Somewhat later a **Rubaiyat of Omar Khayyam** made its appearance in a very lovely edition published by Bryce in 1904. It has V, 59 double pages and measures $2\frac{1}{16}$ by $1\frac{3}{8}$ inches. The binding is in blue or green calf with the upper cover and spine richly gilt-stamped with an oriental design and all edges are gilt. In 1927, Gowans and Gray of London and Glasgow re-published the same edition in large single pages which were not like the earlier edition folded in the middle, thus extending the size of the volume to an oblong $2\frac{1}{8}$ by 3 inches. It is bound in vellum. As late as about 1955, Mr. Gowans sold me a considerable number of the unbound sheets which had lain unused in his house for all these years. Apparently the larger format of this nicely printed edition did not enjoy the same success as Bryce's original much daintier volume.

One of Bryce's most successful enterprises was **The Smallest English Dictionary in the World,** "comprising besides the ordinary and newest words in the language short explanations of a large number of scientific, philosophical, literary and technical terms". The frontispiece shows a portrait of Dr. Johnson. It is usually found with the imprint: Glasgow, David Bryce & Son but can also be encountered with that of Frederick A. Stokes Company, Publishers, New York. The printer is in both cases Robert Maclehose, 153 West Nile Street, Glasgow, the University Press printer. It has 384 pages of very fine, thin india paper and measures approximately (the sizes vary slightly) $1\frac{1}{16}$ by $\frac{3}{4}$ inches. It is bound in flexible red roan and preserved in a hinged metal locket with strong circular magnifying glass set into the top cover. That metal lid bears the engraved inscription: "Smallest Dictionary with magnifying glass" while the lower cover shows a globe. The case has a ring so that it can be carried suspended from a watch chain, etc. There exist also finer and more elaborate

BRYCE'S ENGLISH DICTIONARY. "The smallest English Dictionary in the World". Glasgow, no date. In a metal case with inset magnifier.

lockets, a very attractive one made of much stronger metal with a delightful etched design showing a compass, a bird in flight and leafy sprays. The most luxurious case, also with inset magnifying glass, is made of gold-plated hall-marked silver with the front-cover opening with a swivelling motion. Quite a few of the dictionaries we have seen, bear an advertisement for Pears, the famous soap firm, on the lower cover of the leather binding which is always lettered in gilt on covers and spines. At least one copy we have seen had the inscription "Pearson's Dictionary" stamped on the front-cover.

This miracle of miniature book production is "dedicated by the publishers to Mrs. Kendal in appreciation of kindly encouragement given to the production of tiny articles, of which she has a unique collection". Although the photographic reduction of the printing diminished the size of the letters to about $1\frac{1}{2}$-point, the contents are easily readable with the very necessary help of the provided magnifying glass. It is surprising that although according to Bryce very many thousands of these dictionaries were issued, they are now becoming distinctly scarce and command steadily rising prices.

Two other miniature dictionaries produced by Bryce are **The Smallest French and English Dictionary in the World** by F. E. A. Gasc, M.A. (of Paris) with four unnumbered leaves and 647 pages followed by one unnumbered page, and **A New Pocket Dictionary of the English and German Languages,** dated Glasgow, 1896 and comprising (8), 677 pages. Both were issued in flexible red leather in metal cases and are of the same size as the tiny English dictionary. They are however very much rarer, especially the German one which is reduced from the third stereotype Tauchnitz edition.

The Tourist's Conversational Guide in English, French, German, Italian by Dr. J. T. Loth is, according to Spielmann, No. 355-A "perhaps the rarest of all the tiny Bryce miniature books". It has 126 pages and is in size and binding similar to the other midget dictionaries.

Under the title **Bryce's Diamond English Dictionary** the firm published in 1896 a slightly larger but still very dainty volume of 860 pages, measuring $1\frac{3}{4}$ by $1\frac{1}{4}$ inches which is occasionally found in cloth but more frequently in richly and attractively gilt-stamped red or black leather.

The Bible remains the most widely read book of all. It will therefore surprise no one that fairly early in his career as a miniature book publisher Bryce approached the Glasgow University Press with the request to print for him a complete Bible of very small size. This saw the light of day in 1896 with the joint imprint of Bryce in Glasgow and Henry Frowde, Oxford University Press in London. It has 876 pages printed on the finest india paper and measures on average $1\frac{13}{16}$ by $1\frac{1}{4}$ inches. Many copies were handsomely bound in richly gilt-stamped dark-blue leather with gilt edges and a strong magnifying glass inserted in a pocket inside the lower cover. Other publisher's bindings include blue leather with overlapping sides, black or green morocco marked "silk sewn" inside the front-cover, or red morocco with gilt-tooled inside dentelle and red edges gilt. All these variants have the magnifier inserted in the lower cover.

This, the earliest complete miniature Bible, was reprinted in 1901, the date no longer on the title page as was the case with the first issue but on the licence leaf on the verso of the title. This date which in its original form reads in print eighteen hundred and ninety has been altered in ink to 29th day of March nineteen hundred and one before it was handed over to the lithographers. That issue can be found in blind-stamped cloth with yellow edges, in polished calf with gilt red edges, in flexible black or maroon morocco with richly gilt-stamped front-cover and spine and preserved in a metal case with inset magnifying glass. Other copies were bound in blind-stamped calf of either light or dark brown colour with or without metal clasp and imitating a sixteenth century binding.

The 1901 Bible can also be encountered in dark purple cloth with a metal medallion carrying the photographs of King Edward VII and Queen Alexandra glued to the centre of the front-cover. This latter version was marketed to celebrate the coronation of the Royal couple in 1902. We have also seen a copy in cloth with the gilt-stamped lettering "Souvenir of the Glasgow Exhibition".

A later reprint bound in blind-stamped leather has on the spine the inscription "Coronation Bible" and the date 1911, this time in honour of the crowning of King George V.

During the same year, Bryce and Son, sometimes in conjunction with the Oxford University Press, produced a "miniature chained Bible and lectern" costing 3 shillings and sixpence "for the tercentenary commemoration of the Authorised Version of the English Bible, 1611-1911". This great curiosity which has remained very popular with collectors to this very day, consists of the Bible in its fake renaissance binding affixed to a 5½ inches high wooden lectern by means of a chain which is

THE HOLY BIBLE, Glasgow, 1896. The first miniature Bible published by David Bryce & Son. Binding.

109

intended to be "a facsimile of what may be seen in Hereford and other cathedrals and parish churches all over the country".

Finally, we would like to mention three issues with significant textual additions. The first is **Robert Burns' Family Bible** where between the Old and New Testaments a sheet is inserted stating in very bold letters: "Smallest Bible in the World with Burns' Family Register in the Poet's Handwriting" followed by a separate leaf with the facsimile of that register.

The second is **Shakespeare's Family Bible,** with "Notes of the Family Records, and Facsimiles of the Entries in the Parish Register, Stratford-upon-Avon".

The third is a much rarer and more significant variant with 15 extra pages added to the text of the Bible and an additional title which reads: "Four national anthems (God save the King, La Marseillaise, La Brabançonne, Russian National Anthem). Recessional, by Rudyard Kipling. Evening Prayer of a People, by Neil Munro." We were lucky to find a copy with its original dust-jacket intact, bearing pictures of the Belgian, British, French and Russian flags in colour in front and the words "The Allies' Bible in khaki, 1914" on the

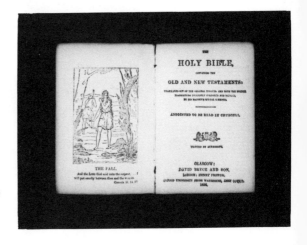

THE HOLY BIBLE. Glasgow, 1896. The first miniature Bible published by David Bryce and Son. Title page.

spine. It is bound in khaki-coloured cloth, weighed one ounce and was priced One Shilling net with magnifying glass, postage 1d.

All the above-mentioned Bryce Bibles are embellished with 28 full-page line illustrations reduced from designs by Charles Bell Birch, A.R.A. (1832-1893) who is chiefly known as a sculptor.

A year before he brought out his complete Bible, Bryce published **The New Testament of Our Lord and Saviour Jesus Christ** in a staggeringly small edition measuring only $\frac{3}{4}$ by $\frac{5}{8}$ of an inch in its smallest form while some larger copies measure as much as $1\frac{1}{8}$ by $\frac{3}{4}$ inches. All copies are dated 1895 and bear the imprint: Glasgow, David Bryce and Son, London, Henry Frowde, Oxford University Press. They are usually bound in dark-blue flexible leather but we have seen copies in red leather wrappers and, very rarely, hardbound in calf. Most of the metal cases with inset magnifying glass are of the same size as those used to house the tiny dictionaries, and are therefore slightly too large. Only once did we see a case in sterling silver of exactly the right size for this the smallest complete New Testament in existence. It is finely and clearly printed in photo-mechanical reduction. On the verso of the half-title we find the following notice: "The publishers beg to thank the Oxford University Press for enabling them to produce in this tiny form a facsimile of their Pica 16mo New Testament, printed on the very thinnest Oxford India paper ever made". The book in its miniature edition is printed by the Glasgow University Press.

The Koran is another almost legendary title published by Bryce. It is entirely printed in Arabic, measures 1 by $\frac{3}{4}$ inches and is generally assumed to have been first issued around 1900. The bindings vary from richly gilt-stamped red or black morocco with gilt edges to plain stiff wrappers and yellow edges. We have seen a lovely copy from the celebrated Vera von Rosenberg collection bound in green morocco with inside dentelle and gilt edges, measuring $1\frac{1}{4}$ by $\frac{7}{8}$ inches. All the copies were issued in the usual metal lockets with inset mag-

111

nifying glass. During World War I many copies were issued to Muslim soldiers fighting with the Allied troops and were often regarded as talismans. Lately it has become increasingly difficult to find copies of this book which thirty years ago was so common that an oriental bookseller of my acquaintance had an entire drawer full of them, selling them at five shillings apiece. The great economic, political and spiritual revival which has taken place in the Arab world may perhaps account for the present scarcity and have led to the absorption of most of the remaining copies.

Another Bryce miniature in a foreign script and without any imprint in the English language is the **Bhagavad Ghita** in Sanskrit, with 11 attractive line illustrations. It measures 1 by $\frac{3}{4}$ inches; bound in richly gilt-stamped red morocco and in the customary metal case, it was probably also

KORAN, in metal case with magnifying glass. Glasgow, David Bryce.

112

published around the year 1900. Copies were always much rarer than those of the Koran.

Devoted as he was to his native Scotland, Bryce published, at about the same time as the two previous titles, a tiny facsimile of the rare first edition of Burns' **Poems, chiefly in the Scottish Dialect,** Kilmarnock, 1786. It measures $1\frac{1}{8}$ by $\frac{3}{4}$ inches. Most of the copies we have seen were in the original printed wrappers, some few however can be found in flexible red leather and with yellow edges, in red niger morocco and raised bands or in tartan boards with silk spine.

Other tiny volumes are: **Golden Thoughts from Great Authors,** selected by Alice Crowther, with the imprint of either David Bryce, Glasgow, or Frederick A. Stokes, New York, but always printed by the Glasgow University Press, with 128 pages and measuring $1\frac{1}{16}$ by $\frac{3}{4}$ inches; **Old English, Scotch and Irish Songs, with Music,** "a favourite selection, edited by William Moodie. With 24 original sketches by A. S. Boyd", 127 pages, same size and bindings as above; **Witty, Humorous, and Merry Thoughts. Selected by T. M.,** same size and bindings, although we once saw a copy of this title bound much more carefully in olive calf with the words "Witty Thoughts" gilt-stamped on the upper cover. The volume comprises 128 pages and exists both with the Bryce, Glasgow and the F. A. Stokes, New York imprint.

Bryce issued the four above-mentioned English titles together with the smallest dictionary jointly under the title "Mite Series in Tartan", preserved in a fitted wooden box with six compartments, one of them occupied by a portrait of Burns covered with a magnifying glass set in a wooden frame and each volume bound in boards of different tartan designs, with red silk spines.

There also exists an edition of Thomas Gray's **An Elegy written in a Country Churchyard,** published by D. Bryce and Son in Glasgow in 1911, comprising 96 pages and measuring only $\frac{11}{16}$ by $\frac{1}{2}$ of an inch, bound in green gilt-stamped leather. It is exceedingly rare and was at one time said not to exist, despite a detailed announcement about its publication issued in a special leaflet. We have seen a copy and Ruth Adomeit describes the book in her possession in the *Miniature Book Collector*.

Bryce's greatest achievement as a leading promoter of miniature books which gave great encouragement to the collectors in that field was undoubtedly the issue of the various literary sets or individual volumes "dedicated by special permission to Miss Ellen Terry", the great English actress.

All the volumes in the "Ellen Terry" series measure approximately $2\frac{1}{8}$ by $1\frac{1}{2}$ inches and can be found in all kinds of bindings ranging from cloth with or without onlaid decorative celluloid plaques, to chamois leathers of various colours, finely gilt-stamped calf or beautiful morocco covers of different hues, with colours occasionally deliberately mixed within the same set for better effect. We have also seen volumes with embossed hall-marked silver plaques affixed to the front covers. Some volumes have untreated, others red or gilt edges, some are lettered in gilt on upper covers and spines while others have gilt paper lettering pieces. The paper on which the text is printed varies from quite thick leaves to the finest and thinnest india paper.

The most prodigious of these sets is the 40-volume edition of Shakespeare's Works, comprising the plays, the sonnets, a biographical sketch and a glossary. It is edited by J. Talfourd Blair, each volume has an attractive frontispiece and the type used is clear and not too small to be read with the naked eye. Most editions bear on the verso of the title pages the imprint: "Printed at the University Press, Glasgow, MCMIV", (1904), while that on the recto reads: "Glasgow, David Bryce and Son. London: Henry Frowde, Oxford University Press Warehouse, Amen Corner" with the O.U.P. address printed in smaller type to emphasize the pre-eminence of Bryce as the publisher. Other editions, also dated 1904, replace the Oxford University Press imprint by that of Frederick A.

Stokes of New York. A different imprint altogether is "Andersons, Edin. Ltd., Printed in Scotland" or "Andersons, Edinburgh, Limited" with "Made in Scotland" on the verso of the title. While these editions are identical in text to those bearing the Bryce imprint and are still dedicated to Ellen Terry, they are undated and obviously a good deal later than 1904.

The sets are housed in attractive swivelling bookcases made of oak, their size varying according to the thickness of the individual volumes which varies from over $\frac{1}{2}$ inch for the cheapest cloth-bound editions to circa $\frac{1}{4}$ inch for the leather-bound thin paper volumes. We have also seen a very fine mahogany case with a star-like ornament in lighter-coloured wood inlaid into the top which served to house the beautiful luxury edition bound in straight-grained red morocco with gilt fillets and a coat of arms gilt-stamped on all front-covers. Yet another shorter set consisting of **Hamlet, Julius Caesar, The Merchant of Venice, Midsummer Night's Dream** and the **Tempest,** finely bound in black morocco, was issued in a wooden stand with attractively designed end in sterling silver.

Another important set issued by Bryce in conjunction with the Oxford University Press is a four-volume edition of Tennyson, published in 1905. It consists of **English Idylls and other Poems,** 383 pages, **Idylls of the King & other Poems,** 384 pages, **In Memoriam, and other Poems,** 384 pages, and **The Princess & Maud,** 319 pages. These volumes were issued singly, and also in a dark-green case made of cardboard and wood held together by a well-designed silver frame. The Tennyson exists also in one volume combining the four individual volumes mentioned above, bound in green cloth or in morocco, lettered on front-cover and spine in gilt "Poems by Tennyson". That one-volume edition is rare and has XIV, 1472 pages.

Gray's **Elegy in a Country Churchyard & other Poems,** of which we have already mentioned the elusive tiny edition, was also issued in the

"Ellen Terry" size. It is dated 1904, has 384 pages and can also be found with the Frederick A. Stokes New York imprint.

A much rarer volume is **Napoleon's Book of Fate** with portrait of the Emperor and a folding table of the "oraculum". Published in Glasgow by David Bryce and in New York by F. A. Stokes, it was like the other volumes in this series printed by the Glasgow University Press. Dated 1905, it is stated to belong to the "Ellen Terry Miniature Library" and has 79 pages followed by 16 advertising pages.

Robert Burns' **The Cottar's Saturday Night and other Poems,** with line illustrations, is more frequently found with the imprint: Andersons, Edinburgh, and is usually bound in colourful tartan cloth. It has X, 372 pages.

The Ellen Terry Library also includes **Evangeline. A Tale of Arcadia** by Longfellow, of which Spielmann, No. 354 lists a copy with the imprint: Toronto, The Copp Clark Co. Limited and dated 1908, printed by the Glasgow University Press. It has 256 pages, followed by 6 pages advertising "other volumes in the Ellen Terry Miniature Library", and is illustrated with 12 full-page pictures.

Sir Walter Scott's **The Lady of the Lake. A poem in six cantos** of 508, (2) pages completes the series. We have seen copies with the combined Bryce and Frederick A. Stokes imprint and with that of Andersons in Edinburgh, both dated 1905.

Such a prodigious list of miniature books of high quality, to which we must add **My Tiny Alphabet Book** mentioned earlier in chapter nine, clearly demonstrates the wide range of Bryce's interests which embraced religion, linguistics, great literature and juvenilia. His contribution to the totality of miniature books has been of the greatest significance and we do not hesitate to describe the Glasgow publisher as a giant towering over the world of dwarf books.

CHAPTER FOURTEEN

THE OXFORD UNIVERSITY PRESS, EYRE & SPOTTISWOODE & OTHERS

It is significant that a press of almost unparalleled prestige in the publishing field such as the Oxford University Press should have been so heavily engaged in the production of miniature books. We have already referred to some joint enterprises in conjunction with Bryce of Glasgow. Simultaneously, it embarked on the creation of a series of uniformly designed volumes bearing its own imprint, the **Oxford Miniature Editions.** The size of the books is $2\frac{1}{8}$ by $1\frac{7}{8}$ inches and they were issued in various bindings in cloth, suede leather and morocco with gilt edges or red edges gilt. As to their texts they constitute a mixture of prestigious literary and religious works, with a practical ready-reckoner thrown in for good measure.

The highlights in this finely printed series are undoubtedly the Bunyan, Goldsmith and Walton all of which are scarce. The details are: John Bunyan's **The Pilgrim's Progress** "from this World to that which is to come", edited by Edmund Venables. London, Henry Frowde, printed at the University Press, 1896, 2 volumes in one, 452 & 418 pages, with frontispiece and line illustrations; Oliver Goldsmith's **The Vicar of Wakefield** published from ca. 1896 to 1905, the earlier editions London, Henry Frowde, the later ones London, Horace Hart, 584 pages, with portrait frontispiece; Izaac Walton's **The Compleat Angler, or the Contemplative Man's Recreation,** "being a discourse of rivers, fish-ponds, fish and fishing", reprinted from the fifth edition, London, Henry Frowde, ca. 1900, XX & 588 pages, with portrait, pictorial title and text illustrations reproduced from the 17th century edition.

The other titles in the series are: Thomas à Kempis' **Of the Imitation of Christ,** 1895, with frontispiece, 576 pages; **The Book of Common Prayer,** "according to the use of the Church of England, together with the Psalter", ca. 1896 to 1905, frontispiece and 688 pages; **My Morning Counsellor.** "Holy Scriptures arranged as Morning Meditations for Edification, Guidance and Comfort", 1900, 767 pages and one advertisement page; **My Evening Counsellor,** 1900, with 767 pages; **The Christian Year.** "Thoughts in Verse for the Sundays and Holydays throughout the Year", a reprint of a book originally published in 1827, no date but 1896 or earlier, with frontispiece and 480 pages; **The Thumb Ready Reckoner,** "Interest & Discount Tables, British and Foreign Weights and Measures, The Metric System, Foreign Money, Postal Guide, &c.", 1895, with 640 pages.

The above-mentioned nine volumes, all printed very well indeed in 6-point type, can be found gathered together on an attractive hall-marked silver stand.

Other O.U.P. titles are **The Thumb Note Book** containing 384 pages of blank paper for ms. notes, together with a calendar to the end of the century (the 19th), interest, discount and wages tables, metric system, foreign money, foreign words and phrases, etc., the printed section of the little volume comprising 96 pages. The book is dated 1896. We have also seen **The New Testament of Our Lord and Saviour Jesus Christ** and **The Book of Common Prayer** in the curious "finger size", both measuring $3\frac{9}{16}$ by $1\frac{3}{16}$ inches, the format described by the publishers as "brilliant 96mo", with the small brilliant type being used for these titles.

Much appreciated by collectors is a 5-volume set of Charles Dickens' **Christmas Stories,** of the same size as Bryce's "Ellen Terry" edition, each volume measuring circa $2\frac{1}{8}$ by $1\frac{1}{2}$ inches and obviously published in collaboration with Bryce, although his name does not appear in the imprint which reads: London, Edinburgh, Glasgow, New York and Toronto, Henry Frowde or Horace Hart, 1904. Some issues are dated 1906. The bindings vary a great deal and include buckram, suede leathers of different colours, morocco or silk. We have seen sets with the portrait of Dickens gilt-stamped on the upper covers, others with sterling silver plaques attached to the front-covers, a particularly beautiful one, with an embossed street

118

scene outside an inn showing people drinking and a fiddler playing music. The sets were also issued with little silver stands or a leather case with a celluloid window on top showing the titles which could be closed with a metal clasp.

The five titles are **The Battle of Life,** 368 pages; **The Chimes,** 368 pages; **The Cricket on the Hearth,** 390 pages; **A Christmas Carol,** 350 pages; **The Haunted Man, and The Ghost's Bargain,** 410 pages. Each of these volumes has eight illustrations with the exception of the **Christmas Carol** which has seven. Once or twice we have come across copies with the imprint of Chapman and Hall, but in all other respects identical with those bearing the Henry Frowde imprint.

Another set modelled on the "Ellen Terry" prototype is a 5-volume edition of selections from the work of Washington Irving, published by Thomas Y. Crowell & Co. in New York and printed by the Riverside Press, Edinburgh, circa 1905. Other copies are published by George Harrap

THE HAUNTED MAN ...
by Charles Dickens. London,
Henry Frowde, 1904. Title
page.

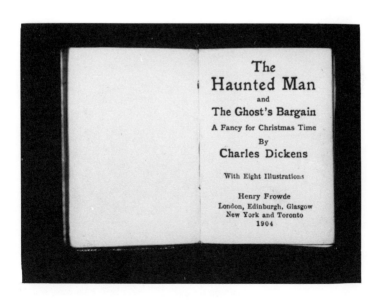

in London, and printed by the same press as the Crowell set. The volumes measure about $2\frac{1}{8}$ by $1\frac{1}{2}$ inches and are bound in suede, polished calf, or gilt-stamped vellum boards, with gilt edges. The titles are: Selections from: **Tales of a Traveller,** 347 pages; **The Alhambra,** 352 pages; **Bracebridge Hall,** 352 pages; **The Sketchbook,** 383 pages; **Christmas Sketches,** 352 pages. This set is printed on the finest thin india paper and must be described as very rare.

The famous London firm of Eyre & Spottiswoode are also responsible for a number of excellent miniature books. Of particular interest are their **Poetical Works of Longfellow** and **The Poetical Works of Alfred Lord Tennyson,** the first with XV, 1103 and the second with VIII, 1035 pages printed on thin paper. A third title is **The Imitation of Christ** by Thomas à Kempis, comprising LXX & 570 pages. This "Bijou Edition" is dated 1906 and has a preface by W. J. Knox-Little. The reproduction of a rather sen-

POETICAL WORKS OF LONGFELLOW. Eyre & Spottiswoode, ca. 1900. Original silver cover.

120

timental painting by James Saint, entitled "The Soul's Awakening" serves as frontispiece. The size of these volumes and others mentioned below is about $2\frac{1}{4}$ by $1\frac{7}{8}$ inches. We have seen copies in cloth, suede, moroccos of different colours and in gilt-stamped vellum. Some have gilt edges, others red edges gilt. The Longfellow and Tennyson can be found with front-covers of hall-marked sterling silver, bearing beautifully modelled raised portraits of the poets. The spines are richly and delicately gilt-tooled.

Another title is **The Royal Bijou Birthday Book,** "a Selection from the Poetical Works of Shakespeare, Wordsworth, Hood, Tennyson, Moore, Burns, Cowper, Scott, Goldsmith, Hemans, Byron, Milton", printed in black and red, 377 pages, providing opposite the printed pages blank ones only bearing the dates throughout the year for the entry of people's birthdays. We have seen copies in flexible suede leather, in gilt-stamped maroon morocco but also with front-covers in finely designed silver, including one showing a most attractive scene of a family sitting around a table outside a rustic cottage, drinking and smoking.

"THE LIGHT OF THE WORLD" by Holman Hunt, silver binding, ca. 1900.

Quite rare is **The New Testament of Our Lord and Saviour Jesus Christ,** described by Eyre and Spottiswoode as a Pearl 128mo, of 1034 pages. The only copy we have seen was bound in straight-grained dark-brown morocco and had red edges gilt.

The **Handbook of Practical Cookery** is described in the section on gastronomy.

A few English literary works were published by S. Rosen in Venice in attractive editions, measuring $2\frac{3}{4}$ by $2\frac{1}{8}$ inches, and bound in printed cream-coloured boards with leather ties. Amongst them are **Sonnets from the Portuguese** by Elizabeth Barrett Browning and Dante's **La Vita Nuova** in the translation of Dante Gabriel Rossetti. These volumes were printed in black and red and came out in 1906 and 1907 comprising 104 and 272 pages respectively. Rosen was also responsible for a German edition of Goethe's **Gedichte,** with an introduction by Dr. Franz Gnadenfeld, published in 1906 and comprising 269 pages. Some of the Rosen titles were also issued in identical form with the imprint of Fisher Unwin in London. They include also **The Rubaiyat of Omar Khayyam** in the Fitzgerald version, with illustrations by Guido Maria Stella, of 92 pages. All these volumes have a rather insinuating "art nouveau" character and are designed with considerable care and taste.

Anthony Treherne of London published a fairly similar list of miniature volumes of very much the same size. They called their series "The Waistcoat-Pocket Classics". Some of his books bear the additional imprint of the H. B. Claflin Co. New York. The volumes measure $2\frac{3}{4}$ by $2\frac{1}{8}$ inches, are printed in 8-point and are bound in cloth or leather, including a beautiful tree calf binding with gilt fillets and gilt edges.

Amongst the volumes we have seen are E. B. Browning's **Sonnets from the Portuguese,** 1904 and 1905, 96 pages; Gray's **Elegy in a Country Church-Yard,** 1905, 71 pages; **On the Morning of Christ's Nativity,** 1904, 67 pages; the **Rubaiyat** of Omar Khayyam, 1903 and later dates,

78 pages. Treherne also issued a set of Shakespeare in this pleasantly produced series which was dated 1903 or later dates. We have seen only one complete set of it, attractively housed in a shelved leather case which belonged to the great Charlie Chaplin.

We know of one later complete miniature Shakespeare edition, published like the "Ellen Terry" set in 40 volumes and very similar to it in every respect, except that it was hideously bound in black or red rexine, printed on fairly coarse thick paper and thus misses out on the charm and attraction Bryce succeeded in giving to his sets. The later set was published by Allied Newspapers in London around the year 1930 and issued in a three-tier wooden bookcase. Each volume measures $2\frac{1}{16}$ by $1\frac{3}{8}$ inches. This Shakespeare was issued free to new subscribers to the "Daily Herald" as a propaganda stunt or sold at very low price. To-day I have seen to my surprise sets in their bookcase change hands at as much as £80.

FAUST, by Goethe. Leipzig, Schmidt & Günther, 1907.

CHAPTER FIFTEEN

THE *LILIPUT-BIBLIOTHEK* OF LEIPZIG

One of the most complete series of miniature books devoted to the major literary works of one country is the *Liliput-Bibliothek,* published in the German language by Schmidt und Günther in Leipzig from 1907 onwards. The texts have obviously been chosen very carefully and demonstrate a clear intention to offer to readers and collectors nothing but the best. The volumes are all well printed in an easily legible 7-point type, they measure 2 by $1\frac{3}{8}$ inches and most of them are bound simply but attractively in leather of many different colours. Occasionally they can be found in cloth and we have seen an almost complete set bound in vellum. The paper is invariably of excellent quality and so thin that even the most compendious volumes retain a certain slender elegance. The price was kept at a moderate level. In full leather with gilt edges they sold at Mark 1.50, in vellum at Mark 3 — while leather stands to hold either 6 or 10 volumes and a bookcase of light oak for either 6 or 10 volumes were offered for Mark 1.50 each, a modest outlay which shows that this useful miniature series was intended for the widest possible distribution. The cloth-bound volumes which were issued slightly later, were called a *Volksausgabe* (People's edition) and sold for only 50 Pfennig each. All the books in the *Liliput-Bibliothek* we have seen were printed by Oscar Brandstetter in Leipzig.

The majority of the texts consists of poetry and plays. Johann Wolfgang von Goethe is particularly well represented. Of his plays the following were available: **Faust. Eine Tragödie,** 3 volumes comprising Faust I, Faust II, 1 and Faust II, 2, 1907/8 and later dates, 636, 527, 508 pages; **Götz von Berlichingen,** 1910, 515 pages; **Hermann und Dorothea,** 1907 and later dates, 392 pages; **Egmont,** 1912; **Iphigenie auf Tauris,** 1907, with 302 pages; **Torquato Tasso,** 1908, with 480 pages. There are two volumes of Goethe's poetry, i.e. **Ausgewählte Gedichte,** 1907 and later, 492 pages, and **West-Östlicher Divan,** ca. 1910, with 446 pages. Finally there is his famous novel **Die Leiden des jungen Werthers,** no date, one of the rarer volumes in this set.

Friedrich von Schiller's plays **Die Jungfrau von Orleans,** 1907, with 544 pages, **Maria Stuart,** 1910, with 607 pages, **Wilhelm Tell,** 1907 and later, 495 pages, and **Wallenstein** in two parts, comprising "Wallensteins Lager. Die Piccolomini" and "Wallensteins Tod", 1908, with 594 and 611 pages, and his selected poems, **Ausgewählte Gedichte,** 1907 or 1908, with 509 pages, makes Schiller the second most honoured author in the *Liliput* series.

The other plays in the Library are **Des Meeres und der Liebe Wellen** by Franz Grillparzer, the celebrated Austrian dramatist, 1908, with 372 pages, Gotthold Ephraim Lessing's fine drama **Nathan der Weise,** 1907 and 1908, with 616 pages, and finally two plays by Shakespeare in Schlegel & Tieck's translation **Hamlet, Prinz von Dänemark,** 1907 or 1909, with 595 pages, and **Romeo und Julia,** 1909, with 476 pages.

Other verse comprises Heinrich Heine's **Buch der Lieder,** 1907 which during the first year of publication achieved an edition of 22,000 copies, with 448 pages, and **Romanzero,** 1908 and no date, of 418 pages. There are selected poems, **Ausgewählte Gedichte** by Eduard Mörike, 1909, with 476 pages, Ludwig Uhland, and Emmanuel Geibel. **Rosenblätter** by Assim-Agha is a volume of songs and sayings, translated from the modern Turkish by B. Schulze-Smidt, published circa 1910, with 276 pages, and an edition of selected songs by the famous Paul Gerhardt, **Ausgewählte Lieder,** published in 1907 with 411 pages.

The final volume in the *Liliput-Bibliothek* is a dictionary of quotations, **Liliput-Zitatenschatz,** edited by Dr. Hans Günther, issued circa 1912 and comprising 954 pages.

The same publishers and printers were responsible for the immensely popular series of *Liliput-Wörterbücher* (Lilliput dictionaries) of the same size as the above classics, but with very few exceptions bound in red flexible cloth and sold at 90 pfennig each. They are not dated. In one of the volumes we have before us, published around 1910, the publishers state that about 2 million copies were then in circulation, that they contain on average 12-15,000 words and comprise 600 to 1000 pages. Twenty two dictionaries were intended for Germans, 13 *pour les français,* 8 for Englishmen, 8 *pegli Italiani,* 8 *por los Españoles,* 4 *pour les Russes,* 2 *pour les Polonais,* 2 for Bohemians, 2 for the Dutch and 2 for Roumanians. Many of these little books were edited by notable scholars, amongst whom the name of Prof. Dr. F. J. Wershoven recurs most frequently. Other editors were Dr. Lorenzo Gonzales Agejas and D. W. Ganzenmüller.

In the 1960's these dictionaries were revived by the well-known scholarly firm of Langenscheidt under the title of "Langenscheidt's Lilliput Dictionaries" and they state on the verso of the title page that "the term 'Lilliput' is internationally registered as a trade-mark". It is also stated that the dictionaries "are available in more than 100 different editions for all important foreign languages." Bound in flexible crimson imitation leather, the volumes measure 2 by $1\frac{1}{2}$ inches. As places of issue both Berlin and Munich are mentioned on the verso of the titles while in some of the editions the title page itself only mentions Berlin-Schöneberg as the place of publication.

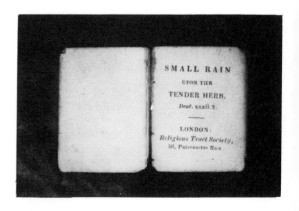

SMALL RAIN UPON THE TENDER HERB. London, Religious Tract Society, Title page.

126

CHAPTER SIXTEEN

DEVOTIONAL BOOKS PUBLISHED BY THE RELIGIOUS TRACT SOCIETY AND OTHERS AFTER 1800

The great religious revival which took place during the 19th century, especially in England, went hand in hand with a flood of devotional books, many of them in miniature format. Some of them were intended both for children and an adult readership. Their number is legion and we can therefore only give a selection of such items, concentrating on those found more frequently or of special interest.

Very popular were the publications issued by the Religious Tract Society in London. As most of them were undated, any dates given here are estimates. A tiny volume, enchantingly entitled **Small Rain upon the Tender Herb,** belongs to the best-loved miniature books and was obviously much treasured by our Victorian ancestors. The first edition appeared in the early 1830's and many subsequent editions were printed at least up to the 39th edition. We have seen an edition which had a specially inserted printed leaf "Portsmouth Soldiers Institute. Anniversary 1890". The size remained more or less constant over the years, $1\frac{5}{16}$ by $1\frac{1}{8}$ inches. The earlier editions were finely printed by C. Whittingham at Chiswick, the 29th edition was still printed by Whittingham in association with Wilkins while the latest issues we have seen were printed by Spottiswoode & Co. The type used is 5-point. The contents consist of short Bible extracts for every day of the year and even include the 29th of February. The bindings vary a great deal but the majority of the earlier volumes are in wallet-shaped red morocco with flap to close, and gilt edges. They also occur in maroon morocco, in red, maroon or green morocco boards with gilt fillets and four gilt lines on the spine, sometimes within leather cases with the insides lined with pink paper. The top quality bindings, obviously destined for special occasions, have silver clasps and endpapers of watered silk.

A very similar volume, specifically intended for juveniles, is **Children's Bread; or Daily Texts for the Young,** measuring $1\frac{15}{16}$ by $1\frac{1}{4}$ inches, of which we have seen a tenth edition bound in cloth which can be dated about 1850 while the earliest issues must have appeared in circa 1835. A third volume of much the same nature published by the Religious Tract Society and printed by Whittingham or Whittingham & Wilkins is **Dewdrops,** measuring 2 by $1\frac{1}{2}$ inches. Of this title we have also seen a 39th edition which must have come out between 1845 and 1850. The bindings are very similar to those of the **Small Rain.** The American Tract Society of New York published several editions of this title which appeared also under the imprint of Henry C. Sleight in New York and Pierce, and Parker in Boston, as early as 1831.

At the same time when these charming little gems made their appearance, the Religious Tract Society published a considerable number of larger volumes, all measuring approximately $2\frac{3}{4}$ by $2\frac{1}{4}$ inches. The best-known titles are **Gems of Sacred Poetry,** 256 pages, of which we have seen a tenth edition, **Hebrew Lyrics. Select Poems on Old Testament Subjects,** dated 1837, of 252 pages, **Daily Food for Christians,** 96 leaves, of which Spielmann lists a 25th edition, **Daily Prayers and Promises from the Holy Scriptures, Prayers or Meditations of Queen Catherine Parr, printed 1546, reprinted 1831, The Nature and Design of the Lord's Supper and the Obligations of Christians to its Observance,** of 123 pages, the very popular **A Threefold Cord,** of which we have seen a 33rd edition, **Gleanings from the Holy Scriptures, The Proverbs: Translated out of the original Hebrew** and a number of similar titles. They are usually bound in maroon leather, often in wallet shape with **flap** to close, and have gilt edges. Many were printed by Whittingham at his famous Chiswick Press. Some like the **Gems of Sacred Poetry,** have attractive engraved frontispieces and titles and we have seen copies of that title with two extra leaves showing in gold-coloured lithography a basket of fruit and a sheaf of wheat.

Several of these devotional texts exist in American editions. For example we have seen a fine copy of **Daily Food for Christians** in a "fifth

American from the Eighth London edition", published by Tappan, Whittemore & Mason in Boston in 1850 with a frontispiece and 3 fine plates. Houghton, No. 65 lists another edition of that title, published in Portland by Sanborn and Carter in 1846.

While we have no desire to be complete in our mention of 19th century religious works in miniature, there are some which must be included either because they enjoyed a considerable vogue at the time or because of their inherent interest and quality.

John Wesley's **A Collection of Hymns for the use of the people called Methodists** exists in a number of editions. An early one, dated 1815, was printed in London at the Conference Office by Thomas Cordeux and sold by Thomas Blanchard. It has 536 pages finely printed in small type, and measures $2\frac{3}{4}$ by $1\frac{3}{4}$ inches. Another edition of high quality was published by John Mason in London and printed by Robert Needham in 1831, has 710 pages and measures $2\frac{7}{8}$ by $1\frac{13}{16}$ inches. There are later issues of the same edition, dated 1838, 1839 and 1846. Most of the copies we have seen were bound in red morocco with gilt fillets, gilt lines on the spine and gilt edges.

A very much appreciated religious title was **The Dairyman's Daughter**, "an authentic narrative, communicated by a clergyman of the Church of England". The little volume was published and sold at Christie's Bible Warehouse in London in 1826 and measures $2\frac{1}{8}$ by $1\frac{3}{16}$ inches. We have seen a beautifully bound copy in contemporary red morocco with fine gilt-tooled borders and a centre ornament consisting of two entwined hearts. There are later editions of the same title, printed or published by J. Haddon, London, 1830 and S. Ewins in the same city, 1832, as well as an undated one of circa 1840, comprising 224 pages. They were bound in cloth or roan.

A miniature volume of outstanding quality is **Rules and Instructions for a Holy Life** by Robert Leighton, Archbishop of Glasgow. It was first published by Hamilton, Adams and Co., London, 1833, has 60 pages, a wood-engraved half-title by O. Jewitt, and measures $2\frac{1}{2}$ by $1\frac{3}{8}$ inches. It is excellently printed in small but very clear type by T. Combe and Company in Leicester and was bound in green or blue watered silk with gilt edges. Other editions we have seen are dated 1835 and 1838.

Much loved by collectors is a small series of books published around 1845 to 1850 by C. Duff or G. E. Petter in London, bound in gilt-stamped cloth with gilt edges and measuring 2 by $1\frac{5}{16}$ inches. Not all the titles are of a religious nature. They include **The Life of Abraham,** 120 and (8) pages, **The Life of Alfred the Great,** with engraved frontispiece and title followed by a printed title, 121 pages, **The Life of Christ,** 125 pages, **The Life of Joseph,** 127 pages, with engraved frontispiece and title, **The Life of Samuel,** with engraved title and frontispiece, 128 pages. There followed around 1855 **The Life of the Rev. C. H. Spurgeon, Minister of Park Street Chapel, Southwark,** 126 numbered and 2 unnumbered pages. The series is described by the publishers as the **Diamond Series.** It also includes **The Diamond Text Book,** which we have seen both with the Duff and with the Petter imprint and has 128 unnumbered pages with Bible quotations for every day of the year.

A larger volume **The Christian's Daily Bread** also contains Biblical extracts. It was published by T. Nelson in London and Edinburgh in 1852, 1853 and 1861, has 188 pages and measures 3 by $2\frac{1}{2}$ inches.

In the 1830's **The Epistles of Paul the Apostle** were published in Birmingham, measuring $2\frac{1}{2}$ by $2\frac{1}{8}$ inches. We have seen that to the Galatians, 63 pages, Ephesians, 62 pages, Philippians, 32 pages, Colossians, 32 pages, Thessalonians, 64 pages and Titus, 30 pages. Most of them were published by T. Groom, some by J. Moore.

J. Nisbet of London also published books taken from the Old and New Testament, measuring $2\frac{5}{8}$ by

$2\frac{1}{8}$ inches, most of them bound in morocco wallets with flap to close and with gilt edges. We have seen "Genesis", 1833 with 258 pages, "The Book of Daniel", 1833 with 119 pages, "The Book of the Prophet Ezekiel", 1835 with 260 pages, "The Proverbs", 1832 with 112 pages, "The Gospel according to St. Luke" with 182 pages, that of St. Mark with 108 pages and that of St. Matthew with 167 pages, all of them dated 1835. These volumes can also be found with the imprint: London, Hamilton, Adams & Co.

Towards the end of the century, **The Book of Common Prayer** and **Hymns Ancient and Modern** were published in huge numbers and many of the miniature editions have survived. With only some slight variations, their size is $2\frac{1}{8}$ by $1\frac{3}{4}$ inches. The Common Prayer "according to the use of the Church of England" is most frequently found in the edition printed by the Oxford University Press and published by Henry Frowde in London which was first issued in 1892 and has 688 pages. A similar edition with the Eyre and Spottiswoode imprint has 630 pages. Much rarer is an edition published in Cambridge by the Cambridge University Press and which has 730 pages. Fairly infrequently, the Book of Common Prayer is found in the curious "finger size", measuring $3\frac{5}{8}$ by $1\frac{3}{16}$ inches. One copy we saw of that edition was lettered in gilt on the front-cover: "From the Franco-British Exhibition 1908". With the numerous editions of the Prayer Book there are many variants as to pagination and frontispieces.

Hymns Ancient and Modern for use in the services of the Church. Complete edition was published as a companion volume and printed by William Clowes & Sons in London. It has 861 pages and is frequently bound into one volume with the **Common Prayer.** Both titles can be found singly or as a combined volume in publisher's morocco, occasionally with an attractive sterling silver plaque attached to the upper covers. These special designs are described in the chapter devoted to publishers' bindings.

131

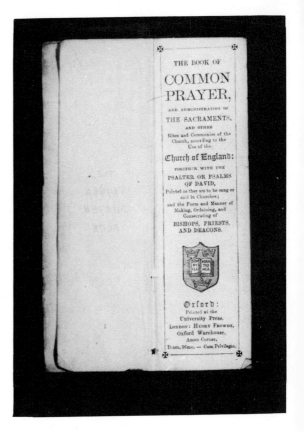

THE BOOK OF

COMMON
PRAYER,

AND ADMINISTRATION OF

THE SACRAMENTS,

AND OTHER

Rites and Ceremonies of the
Church, according to the
Use of the

Church of England:

TOGETHER WITH THE

PSALTER OR PSALMS
OF DAVID,

Pointed as they are to be sung or
said in Churches;

and the Form and Manner of
Making, Ordaining, and
Consecrating of

BISHOPS, PRIESTS,
AND DEACONS.

Oxford:

Printed at the
University Press.

LONDON: HENRY FROWDE,
Oxford Warehouse,
Amen Corner,

Diam. 96mo. — Cum Privilegio.

*BOOK OF COMMON
PRAYER, Finger edition,
Oxford University Press.*

The religious volumes issued by Bryce of Glasgow have been described in chapter thirteen.

In the 1880's the firm of Marcus Ward in London printed a series of "Miss Havergal's Miniature Text Books" which were sold at sixpence each and contain scripture extracts accompanied by verse written by Frances Ridley Havergal (1836-1879) known as an author of religious poems. According to the publishers' description "the pages are exquisitely decorated in colours and each book is tastefully bound in cloth". Measuring an oblong $2\frac{3}{8}$ by $3\frac{1}{8}$ inches, they have invitingly botanical titles such as **Rose Petals, Fern Fronds, Grasses** and **Seaweeds,** indicating the subject of the pleasant colour-printed decorations. The same firm produced **Bible Forget-Me-Nots**. "A Daily Text-Book of Divine Promises", **Bible Heartsease** and similar titles, all published around 1885, printed in colour with floral illustrations and measuring approximately $2\frac{7}{8}$ by $2\frac{7}{8}$ inches.

A hymn book in Welsh language **Y Caniedydd,** (The Singer), was published in Llanrwst, North Wales, by John Jones, circa 1840, measuring $1\frac{3}{4}$ by $1\frac{3}{8}$ inches. It was intended for the use of children in Sabbath Schools. The British Library catalogue lists four other similar miniature books.

Within the compass of this volume it would lead too far to include the very many devotional books published outside Great Britain. Many of them are of limited interest although minibibliophiles may wish to include them in more specialised collections. But no rule is without exceptions. **Diamanten und Perlen. Ein Andachtsbüchlein für Jedermann,** (Diamonds and Pearls, a little devotional book for everybody), is not only a very charmingly produced volume but is remarkable for the geographical spread of its imprint. It was printed and published in 1878 by the Brothers K. & A. Benzinger in Einsiedeln, Switzerland, but mentioning as places of publication New York, Cincinnati and St. Louis as well, thus drawing attention to the connections of the firm amongst German-speaking Americans. The book has a frontispiece produced by photography and measures $2\frac{1}{16}$ by $1\frac{7}{16}$ inches. Another miniature volume issued by Benzinger, J. Wipfli's **Das Gotteskind. Gebetbüchlein für die lieben Kleinen,** (The Child of God, a small prayerbook for the dear little ones) is even more international. Published in 1888 and measuring $2\frac{1}{2}$ by $1\frac{3}{4}$ inches, it mentions on its title Benzinger & Co. in Einsiedeln, Waldshut and Cologne, and the Benzinger Brothers in New York, Cincinnati and Chicago. **Mikrobiblion,** No. 248 lists this rare volume which came into my possession when the Vera von Rosenberg collection came up for sale many years later.

We shall not conclude this chapter without

133

mentioning a number of 19th century religious works printed in Hebrew. One of the most interesting is **Tefillah Mikal Hashana Mincha Katanah,** a small daily prayer book for people emigrating to America, printed in 8-point Hebrew type in Fürth (Germany) by Zürndorffer & Sommer for S. B. Gusdorfer in the year 5615, that is 1855 of our era. It measures $2\frac{7}{8}$ by $1\frac{7}{8}$ inches. Spielmann, No. 191 lists a copy dated 1860. This title, like quite a few others, transcends by far the significance attached to a miniature book simply because of its format; it is an intensely human document carried in their pockets to a new world by waves of European emigrants fleeing from persecution in their native lands.

An extremely rare prayer book according to Sephardi rites was printed in Livorno (**Leghorn**) by Simon Yantilamu in AM 5597, i.e. **AD 1837. Beth Tefillah l'Sephardim** has **200 leaves** and measures 3 by 2 inches. A psalter in **Hebrew** was printed in Pisa in 1863 by Samuel Mulcher, size $2\frac{7}{8}$ by $1\frac{7}{8}$ inches. A prayer book **Sefer Hadras Zekenim,** containing extracts from the Zohar, edited by Jizchak Badhaw was published in Jerusalem by H. M. Salomon in 1885, measuring $2\frac{15}{16}$ by $2\frac{1}{8}$ inches. A prayer book according to Ashkenazi rites, **Siddur Over La-Socher,** useful for travellers, was published by Eliezer Tikozinsky in Bialystok and by Feivel Rosen in Warsaw in 1886, with 424 pages and measuring $2\frac{3}{4}$ by $2\frac{1}{4}$ inches. During the same year a **Siddur Teffilath Israel,** also according to Ashkenazi rites, was printed in Warsaw by Israel Alafin, measuring $2\frac{15}{16}$ by $2\frac{1}{8}$ inches. A **Sefer Seuh Minchah** was published by Samuel Levy Zuckerman in Jerusalem in 1885, comprising 222 leaves and measuring 3 by $2\frac{1}{8}$ inches. It is a rare book containing afternoon prayers with cabbalistic commentary. Frumkin of Jerusalem published in 1899 a **Prayer Book for the Whole Year** according to the rite of Ari, compiled by Rabbi Schneur Zalman of Ladi, the first Hassidic rabbi of the Lubavits dynasty. Its size is $2\frac{13}{16}$ by $2\frac{1}{8}$

inches. A **Haggadah** was issued by the Brothers and Widow Romm in Vilna in 1889, of 64 pages and measuring $2\frac{3}{4}$ by $2\frac{1}{8}$ inches. A tiny facsimile of the Hebrew bible edited by M. L. Letteris was published in Berlin by Menahem M. Shalz in 1896, comprising 605 pages and measuring $1\frac{3}{16}$ by $\frac{3}{4}$ inches. It was issued in a metal case. Most of the Hebrew miniatures are very rare indeed, especially in fine condition, and therefore much sought after.

Of exceptional rarity is **Moral Precepts,** translated from the English into Hindoostany verse, published in Cawnpore (Kanpur), India, in 1834 under the patronage of the King of Oude. It is lithographed throughout and measures 2 by $1\frac{3}{8}$ inches. Besides being one of the first books printed in Kanpur, the elegant little volume is a fascinating example of English proselytizing influence in nineteenth century India.

LE FURET DES SALONS.
Paris, Marcilly, ca. 1825.

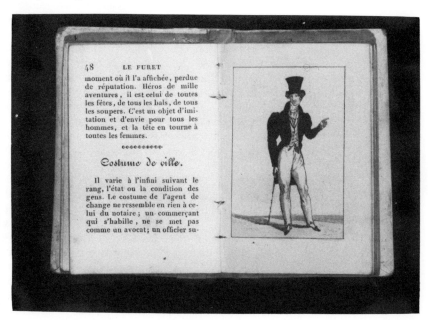

CHAPTER SEVENTEEN

SPECIAL SUBJECTS:

In the following two chapters we are singling out certain subjects for the special attention of miniature book collectors. The wide range of topics which inspired the production of these mini-books is not infrequently closely connected with their portability and waistcoat pocket size. This applied especially to two subjects, erotica and politics, where it may have been important to conceal such books or smuggle them across frontiers. In many other cases, the wide variety of categories is simply a reflection of the all-embracing nature of the human mind. Readers will notice that we are restricting outselves to giving some characteristic examples in each of the categories we have selected. By concentrating on some of the highlights we hope to provide enough incentives for collectors to embark on such rewarding byways.

CARNETS DE BAL

Over the years quite a few of these delightful little dance programmes have come our way. They were intended for ladies to note down the names of their prospective partners during a ball or party. They are not really books, as they consist chiefly of blank leaves of paper or thin ivory which could be swivelled around for use. Many have at least three or four charming lithographed or engraved pictures of dancing couples above the blank spaces left for the insertion of the names of dancing partners. An elaborate *carnet* is listed in the catalogue of the Houghton Sale, No. 51, bound in tortoise shell with gold and silver inlays and pink lining. It was published in Paris, *chez l'éditeur* circa 1830 and measures $1\frac{7}{8}$ by $1\frac{1}{4}$ inches. Quite recently I found an exceptionally alluring little volume, published in Paris at about the same time which besides the obligatory blank leaves has four enchanting coloured plates. The title page, headed *Bal* shows a young man bowing to a young lady while the other plates depict couples dancing a *contredanse,* a *valse* and a *galop.* It measures $2\frac{1}{8}$ by $1\frac{7}{16}$ inches. *Miniature Book News,* No. 29 illustrates many such *bal* items from the extensive collection of Irene Winterstein.

136

COSTUME

Perhaps the most beautiful miniature book on that subject is **Le Furet des Salons,** published by Marcilly in Paris circa 1825; it measures $2\frac{11}{16}$ by $1\frac{13}{16}$ inches, has 128 pages of text and its special glory are the eight finely engraved and splendidly hand-coloured costume plates showing contemporary male and female fashions. **Costüm aus dem Orient** is the title of a pocket calendar for 1839, published by Joh. Bossfeld in Augsburg, measuring $2\frac{3}{8}$ by $1\frac{3}{8}$ inches and illustrated with seven delicately coloured engraved plates of oriental costume. The Budapest University Press published in 1974 a volume entitled **Fashion-Pictures from Bygone Times,** with text by Gyula Kardos in English, Hungarian and Russian, with fashion plates covering the period from 1828 to 1843, meauring $2\frac{3}{16}$ by $1\frac{7}{8}$ inches. Two little items deal with the accessories of costume, **The Crochet Bijou** and **The Embroidery and Alphabet Sampler Book,** the first published by W. H. Collingridge and the second by Groombridge & Sons in London circa 1845, measuring $1\frac{3}{8}$ by $1\frac{1}{2}$ and $2\frac{13}{16}$ by $2\frac{1}{4}$ inches respectively. Both have plates accommodated on folding strips. We have already mentioned Alfred Mill's costume book in our chapter nine.

EROTICA

Besides some crudely produced pictorial alphabets and a collection of equally crude *Mikosch* jokes published in Berlin by Neufeld & Henius circa 1910, 224 pages, measuring $2\frac{3}{16}$ by $1\frac{1}{2}$ inches, and entitled **Die neuesten Mikosch-Witze,** we know of only two well-produced volumes of an erotic nature, both reprinting poems by the French writer Alexis Piron (1689-1773). They are **Ode à Priape** and **Le Chapitre des Cordeliers,** and have each 12 coloured engravings of high quality and extremely free nature. Published anonymously in Paris circa 1935, they measure $2\frac{1}{2}$ by $2\frac{1}{8}$ inches and are beautifully bound in brown crushed morocco with inside dentelle and gilt top edges. The illustrations are quite obviously due to a satirical artist of considerable talent who not surprisingly desired to remain anonymous. Other

137

erotic volumes containing verse by Piron and other similar poets are mentioned in our chapter four dealing with the 18th century.

ETIQUETTE

Quite a few miniature books deal with etiquette, courtship and marriage. One of them combines all three subjects. It is **The Diamond Etiquette for Courtship and Marriage,** published by G. E. Petter in London and by Johnstone & Hunter in Edinburgh around the year 1850. It measures 2 by $1\frac{5}{16}$ inches and has 108 pages. **The Diamond Etiquette for Ladies** published by the same firms and of similar size, has 106 pages. There also exists a **Victoria Miniature Hints on Etiquette,** London, Kent & Co., circa 1850, with lithographed frontispiece and title in gold, green and blue, measuring $2\frac{5}{8}$ by $1\frac{9}{16}$ inches. It was printed by R. Allen in Nottingham. The three above-mentioned titles are all bound in richly gilt-stamped blue cloth.

A more sensationally titled **Cupid's Catechism, or Guide to Matrimony being the Whole Art of Love-Making Taught by Question and Answer** was published by Harris in London circa 1860, 95 pages, measuring $1\frac{15}{16}$ by $1\frac{3}{8}$ inches. A rather humorous German **Hausbüchlein für Eheleute und Ehelustige,** (Little Handbook for Married Couples and those contemplating Marriage), was published anonymously in the early 19th century, measuring $1\frac{1}{4}$ by $1\frac{3}{8}$ inches. The modern women's liberation movement would have strongly disapproved of the sentiments expressed in this tiny volume.

Two volumes belong to this section although they could have been listed in the subsequent one. They are **Bijou Language of Flowers** with charmingly coloured frontispiece, published circa 1840 by Harris Brothers, London, with 118 pages and measuring $2\frac{1}{16}$ by $1\frac{5}{16}$ inches. A similar text is **The Victoria Miniature Language of Flowers,** with a frontispiece showing the Queen and title page, both lithographed in gold and red. The publishers are Kent & Co. in London, the date perhaps 1845 and the size $2\frac{1}{2}$ by $1\frac{1}{2}$ inches.

FLOWERS

There are several miniature books on flowers, some with attractive illustrations, including Book 7 of the "Infant's Library" mentioned in chapter nine. We would like to draw special attention to **La Petite Corbeille de Fleurs,** published by Marcilly fils aîné in Paris circa 1820, measuring $2\frac{1}{4}$ by $1\frac{5}{8}$ inches. It is finely printed by H. Fournier and comprises VIII and 88 pages. The superb eight hand-coloured flower plates are preceded by a beautiful coloured title vignette showing a golden basket filled with a variety of flowers. The text describes many different ones in prose and verse. More recently, in 1977, the Borrower's Press of Jane Bernier in Winterport, Maine, U.S.A. printed, published and bound deliciously in gilt-stamped niger morocco a tiny volume **Wildflowers** in 250 numbered and signed copies. It measures only $1\frac{1}{16}$ by $\frac{13}{16}$ inches and has 18 enchanting hand-coloured etchings of flowers by Jane Conneen.

GASTRONOMY & TOBACCO

The stomach is well served by miniature book authors. Joseph Bentley's **Gems of Health for Young and Old** was published by the author and G. E. Petter in London circa 1860. The book has 64 pages, measures $2\frac{5}{16}$ by $1\frac{3}{4}$ inches and the text is entirely devoted to food and drink, advocating vegetarianism.

Das kleinste Wiener Kochbuch der Welt (The Smallest Viennese Cook Book in the World), appeared in Vienna circa 1900 and measures $\frac{15}{16}$ by $\frac{7}{8}$ of an inch. It is extremely rare and a copy fetched £110 at a London auction sale in 1972.

The most extensive cookery book in miniature is the **Handbook of Practical Cookery** by Matilda Lees Dods, published "in a new enlarged edition" with an introduction on the philosophy of cookery by Eyre & Spottiswoode, London, in 1906. It measures $2\frac{1}{4}$ by $1\frac{7}{8}$ inches, has 69 & 836 pages of text and 50 full-page illustrations. A luxury version was issued with the front-cover in hall-marked silver showing the embossed picture of a kettle hanging over a fire with steam rising from it.

In 1905, **The Tiny Book on the Chafing Dish**

was published in Providence, Rhode Island. It has 298 pages and measures 2 by 1¾ inches. Two years later, Livermore and Knight published in the same city three volumes, simply titled **33 Dinners, 33 Luncheons** and **33 Special Menus,** each measuring 2¼ by 2 inches.

Ruth E. Adomeit, the noted miniature book expert, edited **The Little Cookie Book,** imparting "31 favourite recipes of a minibibliophile". It was published by the Lilliputter Press in Woodstock, Vermont, in 1960 with vignettes by Helen B. Herrick, has 18 and 93 pages, measures $2\frac{7}{16}$ by $1\frac{11}{16}$ inches and 2000 copies were printed.

Lovers of French provincial fare will be delighted to possess **Gastronomie en Périgord,** published in 1966 by Pierre Fanlac at Périgueux. It has 94 pages, measures 1¾ by 1½ inches and gives many recipes of the region renowned for its exquisite cuisine.

THE SMOKER'S TEXT BOOK. Leeds, J. Hamer, First Edition, 1863. Title page.

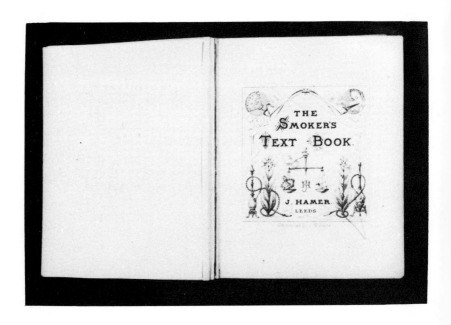

The Smoker's Text Book edited by J. Hamer is a comprehensive anthology of prose and verse on tobacco and smoking, published for the first time by the editor himself in Leeds in 1863 and reprinted under the auspices of John Camden Hotten in 1866 and 1870 and with the Chatto and Windus imprint in 1874, both in London. The volume measures $2\frac{13}{16}$ by $2\frac{5}{16}$ inches and has over 100 pages of text printed in Brilliant 4-point type. The first edition is extremely rare and even the three later editions are not easy to find. One of the most endearing features of this finely produced volume, usually found in its original gilt-stamped cloth with gilt edges, is the engraved title preceding the printed title, showing nargileh water pipes, tobacco plants and, in the centre scales weighted on one side by a crown and on the other counterbalancing it a smoking pipe. The volume is dedicated "to all true smokers of every land and clime".

THE SMOKER'S TEXT BOOK. Leeds, J. Hamer, First Edition, 1863. Binding.

HISTORY & POLITICS

It will be no surprise to anyone to hear that the tiny format has frequently been used for the purposes of historical information and political propaganda. Small pamphlets and books are easily concealed and can be passed on to others without attracting too much attention. Boccalini's famous tract **Pietra del Paragone Politico,** published in Amsterdam and Venice in 1615, though issued in a very small format is still too large for our purposes as are the underground booklets smuggled into Nazi Germany before or during the last war or dropped from planes over enemy territory. There are, however many books which properly belong in miniature book collections. As early as 1814, twelve circular all-engraved discs were issued in Germany which depict and describe various allied battles against Napoleon, including Lützen, Vittoria, the destruction of the First French Army Corps in August 1813, and finally the crossing of the Rhine by the allied armies in December 1813. The discs measure two inches in diameter and illustrate in hand-coloured engravings the battle scenes while giving textual explanations on the verso. The final disc is embedded in the circular lid of a medallion-shaped silver box and states that the year 1813 has ended gloriously for those who fought for a holy cause and have liberated German soil.

The British Library conserves in its miniature book collection two variant copies of **General Cass's Letter to the Harbor and River Convention** which were published in 1848 by the Journal Press in Chicago and the People's Press in New York. Both measure $1\frac{5}{8}$ by $1\frac{3}{8}$ inches, have eight pages of text, a folding facsimile and a humorous erratum at the end which reveals the true purpose of the little volumes by stating: "In the last line in the word Cass the 'C' should be omitted."

About the year 1855, A. S. Petter and J. Blackwood in London published a series entitled "Heroes of the War" with volumes on Sir C. Napier, Sir De Lacy Evans and Lord Raglan, each of 128 pages and measuring 2 by $1\frac{5}{16}$ inches. Like the volumes in Petter's Diamond Series, they are bound in gilt-stamped cloth with gilt edges.

A **Miniature History of England,** lithographed throughout and measuring on average $1\frac{1}{2}$ by $1\frac{1}{4}$ inches, was published in London by Goode Bros. over a considerable number of years. The latest issues must have been published around the year 1910 and have portraits of the English sovereigns from William the Conqueror to King George V, printing at the end his maiden speech, while the earliest, and now understandingly rarest, issues were published around the year 1838 in two volumes with the imprint T. Goode. All the issues we have seen are bound in black or purple wrappers. The quality of the lithographic printing varies a great deal from excellent to the distinctly shoddy.

P.-A. Dormoy, a French officer, had his memoirs of the Franco-Prussian War of 1870/71 published in five volumes under the title **Armée des Vosges: 1870-1871. Souvenirs d'Avant-Garde.** They were published between 1887 and 1890 by L. Sauvaitre in Paris in volumes measuring $2\frac{7}{8}$ by $2\frac{13}{16}$ inches and bound in printed wrappers, comprising 116, 194, 250, 198 and 302 pages. It is unusual to find such a bulky work apparently published only in a miniature edition.

A miniature guide to the composition of the German Reichstag with photographs of all the members of parliament for the period 1898-1903 was written by Joseph Kürschner and published by Göschen in Leipzig, measuring $2\frac{7}{8}$ by $1\frac{7}{8}$ inches.

Around 1895 Franz Huldschinsky in Berlin published **Bismarck-Sprüche,** (Sayings of Bismarck), measuring $2\frac{5}{16}$ by $1\frac{7}{8}$ inches.

A nicely produced volume **A Pocket History of the Ladies of the White House** by Olga Stanley does not only give information about American First Ladies but also about the executive mansion, its apartments, etiquette and social code. It was published in 1898 by the Woolfall Company in New York, has 80 pages and 30 portraits and views and measures $2\frac{3}{4}$ by $2\frac{7}{16}$ inches.

When Theodore Roosevelt was running for

President of the United States, he caused Byron Andrew's **The Facts about the Candidate** to be issued in four languages, English, Danish, German and Yiddish, to cater for the ethnic vote. These volumes were issued by Sam Stone and by the Henneberry Co. in Chicago and measure $2\frac{1}{8}$ by $1\frac{3}{4}$ inches.

Emperor Francis Joseph of Austria made a public appeal to his peoples at the outbreak of the 1914-18 war. It was printed in a tiny miniature volume in 1914, entitled **An meine Völker!**, comprising 47 pages and measuring $\frac{7}{8}$ by $\frac{3}{4}$ of an inch. The binding consists of embossed metal covers, the upper one bearing the emperor's portrait with the inscription "Das Manifest des Kaisers, 28. Juli 1914" on the lower cover. Few copies of this dramatic miniature document appear to have survived.

Three very small books of American historical interest are the **Addresses of Abraham Lincoln,** 1929, with 132 pages, **Extracts from the Autobiography of Calvin Coolidge,** 1930, comprising 129 pages, and **Washington: His Farewell Address,** published in 1932 with 142 pages. They were printed at the Kingsport Press in Kingsport, Tennessee, measure $\frac{7}{8}$ by $\frac{5}{8}$ of an inch and are bound in red, blue and brown niger morocco respectively. The colophon leaf of the Lincoln states that "these miniature editions originated with the students of the Training Division of the Kingsport Press. The initial edition won a first prize at the 1928 convention of the E.B.A. in Boston". A special edition of 150 copies was printed and bound by that training division for the LXIVmos, a group of miniature book lovers. It is of interest to note the printing history of these marvels of superior miniature book production. They were first set in larger type and locked in a forme from which sheets were printed. The photo-engraver then reduced each of the formes photographically until the correct page size for the miniature volume was achieved, then made zinc linocuts for each forme of eight pages. The printers then made nickel electrotype plates and printed the sheets on a Miehle vertical press. Special machines were used, mainly operated by hand, to fold the sheets. *Miniature Book News,* No. 39 reprints the full details of the complicated process.

After they came to power in 1933, the Nazis produced a steady flow of miniature booklets which were illustrated with photographs by Heinrich Hoffman, Hitler's official photographer and showed the *Führer* with the army and navy, with German workers, at his mountain retreat, etc. During the Second World War, similar booklets reported boastfully German victories in Holland, Poland, Norway, France, in Eastern Europe and at sea. None of these publications, measuring $1\frac{15}{16}$ by $1\frac{1}{2}$ inches, were for sale; they were given as receipts for donations during the "Winter Help" street collections and thus served a dual purpose, with propaganda being the most important one.

DES FUHRERS KAMPF IN FRANKREICH.
Bilddokumente von Heinrich Hoffman. Cover and inside page spread.

The people in the countries occupied by the National Socialists had to proceed with much greater caution. It is however alleged that the publication of Jens Baggensen's **Kallundborgs Krönike eller Censurens Oprindelse,** issued in 1943 by A. Vejl's Bogtrykkeri in Kalundborg, was intended as a subtle protest by the Danish people against the German occupation. The book measures $1\frac{7}{16}$ by $1\frac{1}{16}$ inches.

The Tragic Bomb by Luis Cabrera published in Mexico City by G. M. Echaniz in 1964, is to our knowledge the first miniature book dealing with the atomic bomb. It measures $1\frac{7}{8}$ by $1\frac{7}{16}$ inches and is bound in gilt-stamped fawn-coloured leather with silver-embossed endpapers. A recent volume, **In Her Birthday Dress** by George Ballance, published by the Gleniffer Press in Paisley, Scotland in 1977, is a sad poem dealing with the terror reigning in Northern Ireland. It has 19 leaves, measures 2 by 2 inches, and was issued in 150 numbered copies.

CHAPTER EIGHTEEN

SPECIAL SUBJECTS:

HUMOUR

A fair number of miniature books contain humorous stories or jokes and their portability must have quite often contributed to the capacity of men or women to amuse their fellows without having to fall back on their own memory.

Amongst such volumes we find **The Little Budget of Wit,** published by Dean and Munday in London circa 1820, with 286 pages, measuring $2\frac{7}{8}$ by $1\frac{13}{16}$ inches; **The Comic Bijou,** issued by Rock Brothers and Payne in London circa 1835 and consisting of 32 finely engraved caricature plates, bound in gilt-stamped black morocco with gilt edges and measuring only $1\frac{3}{16}$ by 1 inches; **The Punster's Pocketbook,** without publishers or date but probably printed in London around 1850, with a lithographed title and 13 very amusing plates, measuring an oblong $2\frac{1}{8}$ by $2\frac{7}{8}$ inches. The Germans published a jocular soothsaying book entitled **Glücks- und Unglücksspiegel mit verjüngter Schönheit ans Licht getretten** (Mirror of Luck and Bad Luck, etc.), published in the fictitious town of Pumbaskirchen in 1816 and measuring $2\frac{1}{8}$ by $1\frac{7}{8}$ inches. The prophecies are arrived at by opening the little book at random. A French joke book **Les Calembours, Plaisants, Facétieux et Badins de M. del'A-Propos, recueillis et publiés par un Farceur,** Paris, *chez tous les Libraires* in 1843, contains facetious and often salacious anecdotes, puns and jokes. It measures $2\frac{15}{16}$ by $2\frac{7}{16}$ inches. **Loidoros, Petit Livre de Médisances** with numerous amusing silhouette woodcuts, was published in Paris by Bethune et Plon around the year 1840, has 145 pages and contains rather barbed and critical sayings and extracts from speeches. Its size is $1\frac{5}{8}$ by $1\frac{5}{16}$ inches.

HUNTING

Messrs. Ackermann, Printsellers, Publishers, etc. published in London circa 1845 **Pictures of the Wynnstay Hunt,** a booklet mentioning places of meeting and containing a cloth-mounted folding plan to guide to such meeting places. It is bound in red silk with the picture of a hunting scene stamped on the upper cover, contains an 11-page booklet printed on pink paper and measures $2\frac{1}{2}$ by $2\frac{1}{4}$ inches. Similar booklets exist for the Belvoir, Cheshire and Quorn hunts.

MINIATURE NEWSPAPERS AND PERIODICALS

A field which has attracted a good number of miniature book collectors but must remain a side-line, are newspapers and periodicals reduced in size from the originals chiefly by means of photo-lithographic processes. Many of these small papers were produced for the owners of dolls' houses and a list of those specially printed for Queen Mary's Dolls' House Library incude *The Times, The Morning Post, The Daily Mail, Punch, Country Life, The Strand Magazine, Tit-Bits, The Architectural Review,* even *The Times of India.* They are all exact replicas of papers previously published in normal size and not specifically and exclusively produced in miniature. Many of the items we have come across were published in order to advertise the publication in question and therefore distributed free of charge. It is not surprising that the *Newsletter of the LXIVmos,* that excellent though short-lived publication devoted to miniature books, produced a tiny facsimile of their number 5, measuring only $1\frac{5}{8}$ by $1\frac{3}{8}$ inches. In her periodical *The Miniature Book Collector,* Vol. I, No. 4, Ruth Adomeit included a small copy of *Life,* dated January 4, 1883, measuring $3\frac{5}{16}$ by $2\frac{7}{16}$ inches. We have seen several tiny propaganda replicas issued by the *Reader's Digest,* notably the issues for March 1953 and January 1954, measuring $1\frac{7}{8}$ by $1\frac{7}{16}$ inches. Jules Charbneau of San Francisco, an ardent collector of all things tiny, used a facsimile of the title page of the *San Francisco Examiner* of February 11, 1939 as the verso of his visiting card which advertised his collection of 28,000 miniature curiosities. James D. Henderson, the notable miniature book expert, published a book **Lilliputian Newspapers** in 1936 (see the bibliography).

148

PRINTING & TYPOGRAPHY

Surprisingly, one of the rarest books in typographical literature appeared only in a miniature edition. It is **Short Account of the First Rise and Progress of Printing,** "with a compleat list of the first books that were printed", published in London by T. Parker Jun. circa 1763 and measuring $2\frac{5}{16}$ by $1\frac{7}{16}$ inches. The Houghton copy sold for £2400.

Bruce's New York Type-Foundry issued a specimen book **Electrotyped Ornaments** in miniature form, dated 1869. Its 24 leaves show 24 different ornaments costing half a dollar each. The attractive designs were intended for trade cards, bill headings, etc. The booklet is very small indeed, $1\frac{3}{8}$ by $1\frac{11}{16}$ inches, probably the smallest type specimen book in existence.

One of the most curious items in all printing literature and at the same time a most unusual miniature book is **Quads for Authors, Editors & Devils,** edited by Andrew W. Tuer and published at their Leadenhall Press by Field & Tuer in London in 1884. Decribed by them as a "midget

A SHORT ACCOUNT ...
OF PRINTING. London, T.
Parker, ca. 1760.

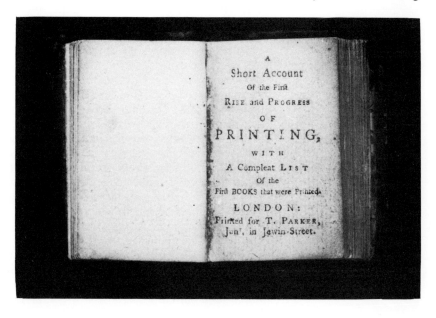

folio", the tiny volume is printed in pearl type on banknote paper of the highest quality, measures $1\frac{5}{8}$ by $1\frac{1}{16}$ inches and has 146 numbered and nine unnumbered leaves. It contains printers' jokes of English and American origin. This small volume is embedded in the scooped-out blank leaves at the end of a larger version of the same book, size 6 by $4\frac{1}{2}$ inches which is lettered on the upper cover "Quads within Quads", followed by the very necessary advice: "In unlocking this forme see that the Quads do not drop out".

Fiori Tipografici, typographical flowers, is the title of an enchanting book of great rarity published by David Passigli in Florence in 1844. It measures $2\frac{1}{2}$ by $1\frac{3}{4}$ inches and the publisher states in his preface to this book of Italian poetry that he charged the brothers Lapi, a painter and an engraver, with the task of illustrating it with 36 wood-engravings, an art which in his opinion reached admirable perfection in England.

A Czech miniature volume devoted to typography is **Pravidla Sazby Typografické,** printed in 500 copies by Vidal Spolek in Prague in 1924, size $1\frac{13}{16}$ by $1\frac{7}{16}$ inches.

Alfred Lubran produced in London at his Nar-bulla Press in March 1969 a tiny booklet of 12 pages which he called **Trial Prints.** It measures 1 by $\frac{7}{8}$ inches and bears the note: "This venture in miniature book making was risked by Alfred Lubran. Produced for the Printing Group of the British Printing Society".

From Gutenberg to Klishograph by Paul Perret is a book published bilingually in English and Hungarian by Budapest's Training Institute for Printers in 1971. It measures $2\frac{1}{8}$ by 2 inches and illustrates on 25 tinted plates the history of printing processes from 1456 to 1947. It was produced in 300 numbered copies not destined for the open market but restricted to collectors' clubs.

SONG BOOKS

The best known English collection of songs has the appropriate title **The Little Warbler.** The earliest dated edition we have seen is that of 1803, published and printed by Oliver & Co. (later Oliver & Boyd) in Edinburgh. The full title is **The Little Warbler; or the Vocal Gleaner, English and Irish Songs.** The volume has 138 pages, the title has the woodcut vignette of a bird, the size is $2\frac{7}{8}$ by $1\frac{3}{4}$ inches. The sequel to this book appeared in 1805 under the title **The Caledonian Siren, or a little Chanter. A choice selection of admired Scottish Songs.** Later editions, published by Oliver & Boyd of Edinburgh, by T. Hughes as well as by Orlando Hodgson of London, by J. Lumsden of Glasgow, and others were considerably extended and comprise as many as six volumes, containing English, Irish, Scottish, Comic, Naval and other songs. Most of the editions we have seen are more or less of the same size as the early edition. Some are furnished with charming or amusing frontispieces and title vignettes. **Hodgson's Little Warbler,** issued circa 1825 has hand-coloured folding frontispieces and coloured titles of a very entertaining character. Joseph Myers & Co. of Leadenhall Street, London, published in 1858 a well produced series of songbooks with the titles **The Fairy Songster, The Elfin Songster, The Peri Songster** and **The Naval Songster,** the last title being "a choice collection of the most popular sea songs and ditties". These volumes are printed in blue in a very small type and bound in plum-coloured, orange, green and blue cloth. Their size is $2\frac{1}{4}$ by $1\frac{7}{16}$ inches and each volume has 128 pages. This series was reprinted in 1871 by A. N. Myers & Co. of Berners Street, London.

FAIRY SONGSTER. London, Joseph Myers, 1858. Front cover.

TECHNICAL REFERENCE

In the case of technical reference books, the miniature format has because of its portability, very significant advantages. **Spon's Tables and Memoranda for Engineers,** compiled by J. T. Hurst, has thus remained a popular work over a long period. The third revised edition for example was issued by E. & F. N. Spon in London and New York in 1878, comprising 140 pages and measuring $1\frac{3}{4}$ by $2\frac{9}{16}$ inches (oblong) and we find that Spon in

151

London and the Chemical Publishing Company in New York were issuing the same title as late as 1941, when the size was $1\frac{7}{8}$ by $2\frac{3}{4}$ inches while the number of pages had been increased to 280. **The Metric System of Weights and Measures** was published early this century by Burroughs Wellcome & Co. in London, Sydney and Cape Town. It has 32 pages and measures $2\frac{7}{8}$ by $1\frac{13}{16}$ inches. Another technical miniature book was issued together with the actual instrument, the use of which it describes. Entitled **Rules, Tables and Formulae for the Patent Circular Slide Rule Halden Calculex,** it was intended "for the use of engineers, architects, surveyors, manufacturers, mill owners, timber merchants, builders, mechanics and all business men". Published by J. Halden & Co. in Manchester circa 1890, it has 95 pages, measures $2\frac{1}{4}$ by $2\frac{1}{4}$ inches and was issued in a leather etui holding both the calculator and the booklet. A recent Yugoslav publication containing hundreds of chemical and physical formulae is **Mini Formule. Matematica — Fizika. Hemija,** by Ahmed & Zoran Kafedzik, in 2 volumes of 224 and 235 pages, issued in 1977/8 by Centar Skenderija in Sarajevo, measuring $2\frac{1}{4}$ by $1\frac{7}{8}$ inches.

TOPOGRAPHY & TRAVEL

London figures prominently amongst topographical miniature books. Besides the children's books published by Boreman, Marshall, Darton & Harvey and Tilt which we have already mentioned, there is a delightful **Bijou Picture of London,** measuring only $1\frac{3}{16}$ by 1 inches with an engraved title and 31 tiny but excellent views of London, issued by Rock & Co. and the same publishers brought out an equally charming **Bijou Picture of Paris** of identical size and make-up, both published at about 1850 and bound in flexible gilt-stamped leather. The rarest of these lovely topographical volumes is **Bijou Illustrations of the United States.** It has 32 plates and also measures $1\frac{3}{16}$ by 1 inches. An unillustrated **Diamond Guide to the Sights of London** was published by the Harris Brothers in London a few years earlier, with 110 pages of text, size $1\frac{7}{8}$ by $1\frac{1}{4}$ inches.

Bijou Illustrations of the Holy Land with engraved title and 31 fine views of Palestine was published at about the same time by J. Hamilton of Philadelphia, U.S.A., bound in gilt-stamped cloth, measuring $1\frac{1}{8}$ by 1 inches.

Lorenzo Benapiani's **Venise. Guide Impressions** with text and illustrations by the author and two coloured plans of Venice was published in 1899 by Bocca Frères in Milan and H. Laurens in Paris. It has 154 pages, followed by 15 pages with interesting advertisements, and measures $2\frac{1}{4}$ by $1\frac{5}{8}$ inches. A feature of this French-language guide, produced by photolithographic reduction at the house of Alfieri & Lacroix in Milan, is a long folding view of the city of Venice.

The ABC, or Alphabetical Railway Guide, January 1929 and **Bradshaw's General Railway and Steam Railway and Steam Navigation Guide** No. 1074 for the 1st month of 1923 are both replicas of the copies specially produced for Queen Mary's famous dolls' house by photographic reduction and measure $\frac{3}{4}$ by $\frac{1}{2}$ an inch and $1\frac{7}{16}$ by $1\frac{1}{4}$ inches respectively. They are both scarce but the quality of the printing is modest. A much finer production is the **Atlas of the British Empire,** also "reproduced from the original made for Her Majesty Queen Mary's Dolls' House", with 12 delightful coloured double-page maps, published by Edward Stanford, cartographers to the King, London, circa 1928. It measures $1\frac{5}{8}$ by $1\frac{3}{8}$ inches and is bound in flexible red morocco with gilt edges. To our knowledge this rare volume is the smallest miniature atlas in existence.

153

CHAPTER NINETEEN

"THE SMALLEST BOOKS IN THE WORLD"

Even in the world of books, records are considered important. We can therefore observe the craving throughout the centuries for ever smaller sizes, the almost breathless pursuit of almost impossible aims. We have already mentioned the famous Dutch **Bloemhofje** in the chapter on the 17th century and the 19th century tiny Galileo and Bryce's minute New Testament. It was left to the present century to carry this process of miniaturisation to absurd lengths and to produce books which are hardly more than specks of dust. Modern technology coupled with unbelievable craftsmanship and superhuman patience have indeed combined to pursue such an advance *ad absurdum*.

This process started — still credibly and with great success — with the printing of **The Rose Garden of Omar Khayyam** by Eben Francis Thompson undertaken by the Commonwealth Press of Worcester, Massachusetts, U.S.A. The book was privately printed in 1932 and measures an oblong 4 by 6 millimetres, $\frac{3}{16}$ by $\frac{7}{32}$ of an inch. This "smallest printed book in the world" was issued bound in hand sewn full crimson morocco and printed on an ordinary printing press; it weighs about a grain and a quarter. 250 sets were printed and sold for $75.00 together with what was called "a definite edition" measuring $1\frac{3}{4}$ by $1\frac{1}{2}$ inches and containing a preface explaining the details of the tiny version. Also included was a proof sheet of the minute volume comprising 4 pages, the so-called "Mother Book" of **The Rose Garden,** measuring 5 by 6 inches and a bibliography entitled "A Thimbleful of Books". These items together with a magnifying glass are contained in a book-shaped box.

The Rose Garden had already been preceded in 1900 by a very small Rubaiyat published by Charles Hardy Meigs at Cleveland, Ohio, a reprint of the text of the fourth edition of Fitzgerald's version. Measuring in its binding $\frac{3}{8}$ by $\frac{5}{16}$ of an inch, it was a giant compared with the edition of the new translation by Eben Francis Thompson published 32 years later. Both these very small volumes can be encountered embedded in the decorative tops of rings specially created for them where they were concealed behind hinged lids. Of these two Omar Khayyam versions the Meigs edition is the rarer one as it was produced in 57 copies only.

Quite a few years later, after the Second World War, Waldmann & Pfitzner of Munich published four very small books, wrongly described as the smallest books in the world, although they were larger than **The Rose Garden,** measuring about $\frac{7}{32}$ of an inch square. The titles are **The Lord's Prayer, I Love You, The Olympic Oath** and **Lincoln's Oath of Freedom.** They were sold together in a plastic case labelled inside "Die kleinsten Bücher der Welt", (The smallest books in the world). Each of the volumes, which were also sold singly, was in turn enclosed in a transparent case of plexi-glass with a strong magnifying glass set into the swivelling lid. The texts were all printed in seven different languages, including English, German, French, Dutch and Spanish. The price was very reasonable and was not more than about £2 for the entire outfit.

The Lord's Prayer by itself with text in Dutch, English, French, German, Spanish, Swedish and an English-American version was sold by the Gutenberg-Museum in Mainz for 10 German Mark to help in the reconstruction of that famous museum of printing. Again, the volume was described by that expert source as the smallest book in the world and the prospectus issued by the museum underlined that the tiny volume was not the result of photographic reduction but that each page was cut by a foundry (said to be in the Netherlands) in metal. The printing and the folding of the pages was said to have been very difficult and each book had been bound in gilt-stamped leather by hand.

In 1971, the East Germans produced yet another "smallest book in the world". It is Egon Pruggmayer's **Bilder ABC. Das kleinste Buch der Welt** published by Edition Leipzig and consisting of 14 leaves, measuring 3 by $2\frac{1}{2}$ mm., circa $\frac{1}{8}$ by $\frac{3}{32}$ of an inch.

155

An even smaller volume, simply entitled **Knjiga**, (Book), was published in Novi Sad, Yugoslavia in 1975, measuring 2.75 by 1.75 millimetre. We have never seen a copy ourselves, although it was printed in 150 copies.

An **Ave Maria** with one illustration, measuring 9 by 9 mm., $\frac{3}{8}$ by $\frac{3}{8}$ of an inch, was published either in Budapest, as Hungarian bibliophiles claim or in Italy as is stated by Italian collectors. It appeared about 1970.

The next time a "smallest book in the world" made its debut it was in Britain in 1978. Ian Macdonald of the Gleniffer Press at Paisley near Glasgow brought out **Three Blind Mice** measuring 2.1 by 2.1 millimetres. This nursery rhyme was set by hand in 4-point boxhead Gothic type on 15 pages which were then engraved on a nyloprint block which was then used to print by hand letterpress on very fine paper. The dried sheets were cut into tiny pages and glued by hand to the case with the aid of dental tweezers. Ian Macdonald wrote to me in August 1978 about "our latest secret project, Three Blind Mice, limited to 45 copies. We are in the belief that this is 'the smallest letterpress printed book in the world' 1978. I am selling these privately at £25 each. I can only offer you ONE copy, sorry". In a later letter enclosing copy No. 12 of this prodigious production, he added that it took him two days to produce one copy. When I ordered additional copies three months later Ian replied: "Alas. All copies are sold. I wish I could make greater output, but my poor eyes." The Guinness Book of Records listed **Three Blind Mice** indeed as "the smallest book in the world" in a special "Stop Press" addendum.

The Toppan Printing Co. Ltd., of Tokyo, Japan, who had been specialising in producing very tiny volumes for some time, issued from December 1979 onwards a "Toppan Ultra Micro Trio", consisting of **Birth Stone, Language of Flowers** and **The Zodiacal Signs and their Symbols,** limited to 500 sets, each volume measuring 2 by 2 mm., competing in size with and slightly beating **Three**

Spine of the Toppan Ultra Micro Books.

156

Blind Mice and described of course as "the world's smallest books", probably with justification. Each volume, if such a microscopic particle deserves to be described as a volume, has 16 pages and the texts are in English. They are accompanied by what is termed as a "Mother Book" measuring 20 by 20 mm., $\frac{13}{16}$ by $\frac{13}{16}$ of an inch, readable with the naked eye and thus giving a clue to the contents of each of the three micro-mini books. The sets were issued in separate cases for each title, each covered in leather of a different colour and equipped with a powerful magnifying glass or placed together in a brass case covered with finely gilt-stamped green leather, housing also the three "mother books" and a beautiful brass magnifying glass attached to a short chain. The micro volumes are kept behind a circular perspex screen which when turned brings one of the tiny books beneath a very small opening so that they can be lifted out if necessary. I recently had the terrifying experience when breathing against the case to see one of the books take off like a speck of dust and it was nothing short of a miracle that I managed to find it again and replaced it in its allotted space.

Another Toppan Micro Book, **The Lord's Prayer,** Tokyo, 1981, ten pages, measuring 1.4 by 1.4 mm, has since been published. Is this going to be the ultimate microbe?

BIRTH STONE, THE LANGUAGE OF FLOWERS and THE ZODIACAL SIGNS. "The smallest books in the World" with magnifying glass. Tokyo, Toppan Printing Co., December, 1979.

157

It can be assumed, at least for the moment, that the Glasgow and Tokyo experiments together with the Yugoslav book and one or two similar ventures in the German Democratic Republic have plumbed the ultimate depths of book production. Technical stunts, together with infinite human patience, have succeeded in producing books which are too tiny to be handled and certainly not worth reading. They have their place in a book dealing with miniature volumes, but I must confess to the feeling that they have a more legitimate destination in the Guinness Book of Records than in a collection of miniature books. Their most legitimate port of call will perhaps be a doll's house where their size may match that of tiny writing desks or bookcases. I can however not conceal the fact that some collectors prize such book microbes above all the other miniature volumes.

Not a book at all and mentioned here only for its curiosity value is **The Smallest Bible in the World,** published by the National Cash Register Company of Dayton, Ohio. It is a 2-page booklet measuring $3\frac{1}{2}$ by $2\frac{1}{2}$ inches in a stiff paper wrapper, containing in an inside pocket a piece of microfilm measuring $1\frac{13}{16}$ by $1\frac{3}{4}$ inches, lettered in gilt "NCR Microimage". The accompanying text states that "the 1245 pages in this edition of the Holy Bible on the attached tiny slide is the result of another scientific achievement by the Research and Development staff of the National Cash Register Company. Each of the 773,746 words of the Scripture appear in this incredibly small space through the use of a newly discovered 'photochromic micro-image' technique. This process makes practical a linear reduction of 220 to 1 which is an area reduction of 48,400 to 1." If ultimate contraction was the chief criterion of what consistutes a miniature book, this would have been the minibook *par excellence.* Luckily this is not the case. Nevertheless this item is listed in the famous Houghton Sale Catalogue of miniature books under No. 321, mentioning that it was produced for guests of the Grolier Club at the New York World Fair of 1964.

Some miniature volumes of an unusual, not to say quirky, nature deserve a special chapter and are worthy of the attention of collectors precisely because they are curious and often startling expressions of the infinite variety in the flights of human fancy.

A German-language **Kalender auf das Jahr 1808** produced in Vienna, with 13 pages and measuring 2 by $\frac{13}{16}$ inches was sold in a slipcase made of marzipan, intended as a Christmas present of a most acceptable edible nature. Similarly the **Mignon-Almanach 1817,** published by Joseph Riedl in Vienna and measuring $1\frac{1}{8}$ by $\frac{3}{4}$ inches was enclosed in a case covered with honeycake. A horrifying contrast to these "sweet" volumes is a copy of **Little Poems' for Little Folks,** a children's book published by Loomis and Peck of Philadelphia in 1847 and measuring 3 by $2\frac{3}{8}$ inches which was bound by P. B. Sanford of Boston in human skin.

To return from disgust to an enchantment which is much more characteristic of miniature books, we would like to mention **Birch Bark Poems 1880** by Charles F. Lummis which were published in Chillicothe, Ohio, U.S.A. in 1882 and consisted of 12 pages finely printed on birch bark, that most delightful though fragile material. The author-printer was the founder of the Southwest Museum and the little volume which went through several 19th century editions, measures $2\frac{7}{8}$ by $2\frac{3}{8}$ inches. In 1969 Karen and Susan Dawson of Los Angeles published a volume by Dudley Gordon on **The Birch Bark Poems of Charles F. Lummis** which measures 3 by $2\frac{1}{2}$ inches. It has a frontispiece printed on birch bark and contains two original leaves of the earlier edition.

An intensely moving miniature curiosity is "The Lord's Prayer, printed in Hyde Park during the Grand National Jubilee 1814 to celebrate Peace" which was finely engraved and printed in the open air on a small silk mat. The engraved portion consists of a wreath $1\frac{3}{4}$ inches in diameter inside which the words quoted above in inverted commas

159

are engraved. They surround a multipronged star within which the "Lord's Prayer" is engraved in such tiny script that it is only legible by means of a strong magnifying glass. The inner circle within which the prayer is contained has a diameter of only half an inch.

La Lanterne Magique published by Marcilly in Paris circa 1825 and measuring $2\frac{9}{16}$ by $2\frac{1}{16}$ inches, consists of 12 separate folders united in a slipcase. Each folder has four pages consisting of the title, two printed and one blank page; within a "magic" coloured illustration is loosely inserted which when held against the light reveals additional subjects adding to or completing the picture. For example *le sorcier*, the sorcerer, produces a beautiful lady previously invisible behind a curtain, *le cauchemar*, the nightmare, shows a barebosomed lady lying in bed who when the card is illuminated from behind has a long-tailed devil sitting on her chest. In *le tombeau*, the grave, we see a soldier in uniform kneeling at a grave while the magic figures conjure up the Emperor Napoleon rising from the dead.

Robert E. Massmann, a most inventive American academic and miniature book maker, took up this idea 150 years later and published in 1977 in New Britain, Connecticut **Magic Nursery Rhymes** with hand-coloured plates which when seen against a light source reveal additional features previously invisible. This was issued in 500 numbered copies and measures 2 by $1\frac{3}{8}$ inches.

A lucky charm consisting of a folding strip with 13 illustrations and 14 pages of French text was published in Rome by Kufon Unione Italo-Belga Aluminio circa 1935, preserved in an aluminium case with ring to suspend on a watch chain or necklace. It measures $\frac{7}{8}$ by $\frac{5}{8}$ of an inch and the illustrations show a hunchback, a pig, St. George and the dragon, a spider, a horseshoe, etc., while the text explains that the 13 figures add up to a much fancied oriental talisman and will protect the wearer against the torments of life.

An odd combined title is **A Calendar for 1840 and Treatise on Indigestion,** published by John

King in London in blue wrappers, with 55 pages of text, measuring $2\frac{1}{4}$ by $1\frac{15}{16}$ inches. The text reveals this miniature book as a publicity effort describing at some length the symptoms of indigestion and then praising a cure effected through taking Babington's Elixir of Rhubarb, sold in bottles by J. King, the publishers of this curiosity.

Phrénologie des Dames, published by L.-B. Salleron in Paris in 1843 and measuring $1\frac{9}{16}$ by $1\frac{1}{16}$ inches, explains twelve different beauty spots on the faces of ladies and their meaning as to the character and disposition of the women in question.

Dictionnaire d'Argot ou la Langue des Voleurs Dévoilée, "contenant les moyens de se mettre en garde contre les Ruses des filous" was published *chez tous les libraires* in Paris circa 1820, has 256 pages and measures $2\frac{13}{16}$ by $2\frac{1}{16}$ inches. I encountered this rare and unusual volume which contains not only a dictionary of thieves' slang but also advice of how to protect yourself against the ruses of crooks, in the fine miniature book collection of the British Library.

Two tiny volumes are housed in cases made to look like matchboxes. The first is **London Characters** with coloured pictures by John Hassall and verse by Jessie Pope. Published in London in 1904 by Grant Richards, it has 103 pages with many delightful full-page illustrations of London trades and professions and measures $2\frac{1}{4}$ by $1\frac{1}{2}$ inches. Printed on very thick paper, the leaves are held together by a slipcase which for no apparent reason is designed exactly like a matchbox. There is much more justification for such a get-up in the second such item. It is a collection of often very crude jokes in German language, **Die neuesten Mikosch-Witze** which we have already mentioned in the erotica section of chapter seventeen. Published circa 1910 by the Berlin firm of Neufeld & Henius, it has 224 pages and measures $2\frac{3}{16}$ by $1\frac{1}{2}$ inches. It is bound in printed wrappers and preserved in an imitation matchbox the label of which reads "Eine Kiste neuer Humor. Zündende Mikosch-Witze mit Schwefel und Phosphor", (A

161

boxful of new humour, incendiary Mikosch jokes full of sulphur and phosphorus). Mikosch was a legendary Hungarian whose highly dubious jokes were intended exclusively for male society.

Two most unusual miniature books are Japanese telephone books measuring $2\frac{5}{8}$ by $1\frac{7}{8}$ inches which were given by geisha girls to their clients. One contains the numbers of theatres, actors, dance teachers, wrestlers and taxicab ranks in Tokyo and Yokohama while the other gives those of restaurants in those two cities.

Marjorie Palmer's book on **1918-1923, German Hyperinflation,** published in 1967 by The Traders Press in New York and measuring $2\frac{15}{16}$ by $2\frac{5}{8}$ inches, is remarkable because its trade binding consists of boards covered with an actual German banknote of the inflation period.

Towards the end of the 19th century cinematic "flick books" made their appearance in the miniature book world. One of the earliest of these moving picture items is **Gies & Co.'s Living Photograph. A Story without Words. The Yankee Cop.** The book was issued by M. Kingsland in 1897 without any indication of place. The publishers' instructions state: "Draw thumb over top edge and pictures will appear as if alive. The pictures are taken by special photographic machinery invented by us." The lively action shows a man being attacked by a robber and a policeman coming to his rescue. A similar item, also dated 1897, is called **Living Pictures. A Story without Words. Champion of the World Robert Fitzsimmons, Carson, Nevada, March 17 1897.** While the first item measures $2\frac{5}{16}$ by $1\frac{1}{2}$ inches, the second is $2\frac{1}{8}$ by 2 inches and shows cinematic scenes from the boxing match. The title page is decorated with a photograph of the world champion.

The Illustrated Bible; also Verses entitled Railway to Heaven deserves mention in this chapter because of its eccentric title. It was published by T. Goode in London over quite a long period during the second half of the 19th century. It has rather crude lithographed illustrations and measures $2\frac{3}{8}$ by $1\frac{5}{8}$ inches and is in black or dark violet gilt-stamped wrappers, often with gilt edges. The first lines of the poem in question are: "O what a deal we hear and read, about railways and railway speed, of lines which are or may be made, and selling shares is quite a trade. Allow me as an old divine, to point you to another line, which does from earth to heaven extend . . .".

Like larger volumes miniature books are of course found in all kinds of bindings ranging from the humble printed wrapper to the most beautiful jewelled gold, silver filigree or tortoise-shell binding. We would like to draw the attention of collectors to some of the more interesting bindings issued or commissioned by the publishers.

The long series of **The London Almanack** published by the Company of Stationers occupy an eminent position in that respect. In many ways they can serve to illustrate the history of bookbinding and the ever changing taste influencing that craft, especially as far as the British capital city is concerned. The earliest issues were usually bound in black or red gilt-tooled morocco and closed with silver or brass clasps. Towards the end of the first half and the beginning of the second half of the 18th century they can be found in white or pink silk bindings, beautifully painted in the then very popular oriental, and especially Chinese, style in very delicate colours, showing flowers, ornaments and domestic scenes. Many of these volumes are also distinguished by the use of fine "dutch" floral endpapers in gold and colours, and they were issued in sharkskin or tooled leather slipcases to protect the delicate silk. A few years later the Venetian style became very popular and such bindings were artistically designed and executed with multi-coloured leather onlays. Almost all of these were issued in matching slipcases. Occasionally the beauty of the earlier London Almanacks is further enhanced by their being placed inside delicately designed silver or even gold filigree cases with chased clasps who are said to have been created chiefly by Portuguese craftsmen who had emigrated to England.

Most of the lovely tiny almanacs published in France from before the Revolution to the middle of the 19th century are distinguished by tooled bindings in black, citron or green but much more frequently in red or maroon morocco, decorated in gilt with floral, bird or arabesque designs, usually within gilt fillets or more elaborate borders and with gilt edges.

Some of the charming illustrated almanacs published in Vienna during the flourishing years of the late 18th century and in the early eighteen hundreds have lovely enamelled covers decorated in colour with animated scenes and often rather allusive texts. Inside the covers mirrors are not infrequently fixed in finely tooled settings.

The Dutch **De kleine Tijdwyzer** is normally encountered in richly gilt-tooled moroccos, sometimes they are also painted in colour showing homely domestic or outdoor scenes.

Pickering's "Diamond Classics" are famed not only for the beauty of the tiny type and the quality of their texts but also because these publishers started in England the fashion of issuing books in cloth. The Horace of 1820 has the reputation of being the first English volume bound in publisher's cloth.

In the presentation of miniature books Albert Schloss in London reached a high degree of sophistication. The English Bijou Almanacs over the publication of which he presided were issued in delicately coloured and gilt-stamped flexible boards, in elegant and splendidly decorated morocco or vellum bindings, always protected by matching slipcases. To keep these highly vulnerable tiny treasures safe, Schloss produced elegant fitted cases covered with the finest velvet or morocco, often lined with white silk and in the publisher's own words "elegantly illuminated and beautifully gilt". They are closed with brass clasps or held together with spring fastening. Almost without exception the cases provided a space to house "a powerful microscopic eyeglass of half an inch focus in tortoiseshell" or in some of the even more luxurious outfits that magnifying glass folded into a mother-of-pearl or silver handle. One of these "jewel cases" we have seen had a finely engraved portrait of Prince Albert fitted into the lid. Many years ago we purchased in the then world-famous jeweller's shop called "Cameo Corner" a unique copy of the 1841 edition of the **Bijou Almanac,** the cover stamped in gilt with a crown and the letters "PR", preserved in heart-shaped mother-of-pearl case and containing a magnifying glass of mother-of-pearl and gold. This was later identified as "the first book presented to the Princess Royal of England" who was then a small child. We purchased that great miniature treasure from Moyshe Oved, a renowned Bloomsbury jeweller, for a modest sum and it lives now, after having passed through the Spielmann collection, in the prodigious Edison collection. It is depicted and described in Iain Bain's book on **Albert Schloss's Bijou Almanacs.**

ENGLISH BIJOU ALMANAC. Schloss, 1840, in its velvet box lined with silk and velvet, with a magnifier.

166

Of considerable interest are the various embossed and hall-marked silver plaques affixed to the front-cover of a number of morocco-bound miniature books issued towards the end of the 19th and the beginning of the 20th century. They are usually found on **The Book of Common Prayer** printed at the Oxford University Press, or the same title published by Eyre & Spottiswoode, as well as on the bindings for **Hymns Ancient and Modern** printed by William Clowes & Sons. The design most widely used for these silver covers is that showing five angels' heads surrounded by clouds, based on a work by Joshua Reynolds. Much rarer is a splendid composition based on Holman Hunt's celebrated painting "the Light of the World". Other silver plaques show the Lamb of God, the sacred initials I.H.S. intertwined to form an attractive monogram, a simple flower stalk, or leafy sprays and flowers with a shield-like panel in the centre. The most elaborate of these silver bindings depicts a horse-drawn carriage pulling up in front of a church. Recently we saw for the first time

Typical miniature volumes, including Schloss's ENGLISH BIJOU ALMANAC, the tiny modern SERMENTS D'AMOUR, Bryce's KORAN, two early 19th century French almanacs, and a half-sized LONDON ALMANACK (with metal clasp).

an attractive silver plaque on **The Royal Pocket Diary and Engagement Book for 1905,** published by Eyre and Spottiswoode which shows an elegant young woman in contemporary dress in front of a landscape.

Of particular interest are the two silver covers provided for some copies of Longfellow's and Tennyson's Poetical Works, published by Eyre and Spottiswoode, with splendid and very striking embossed portraits of the poets.

Fromme's Wiener Portemonnaie Kalender produced by the firm of Fromme in Vienna from the 1890's to the mid-nineteen-thirties is an outstanding example of enterprise and originality in the creation of miniature book bindings. The 1894 edition has either an edelweiss or a four-leaf-clover in silver affixed to the front-cover, the leather binding of the 1893 issue has a gilt-stamped picture of a cat standing on its hindlegs looking longingly at a birdcage; in 1895 the decoration consists of a pinchbeck ornament with inset turquoises or alternatively of a miniature photograph in a circular frame showing a lady, a uniformed guard and a child sitting on a bench. The 1897 almanac has both covers in pinchbeck, the upper one engraved with an imperial eagle, the lower one with a bouquet of flowers. In 1907 there was a binding signed by J. Silberberger of Vienna consisting of violet crushed morocco with a silver ornament in the "art nouveau" style style affixed to one of the corners. In 1927 Fromme used a watered silk binding with tortoise-shell onlay to which a steel ornament with blue enamel decor was affixed. The 1928 calendar is bound in chamois leather with mother-of-pearl corners, a spider's web gilt-stamped on the upper cover and a small metal spider affixed to the centre. "Art deco" has influenced some of the other bindings which altogether splendidly reflect the changing taste around the turn of the century.

CHAPTER TWENTY-TWO

THE MINIATURE BOOKS OF TODAY AND TOMORROW

It is impossible to give within the framework of this book an exhaustive account of present day miniature book production and all the developments earlier this century which led up to it. Our selection from the abundant material available will take account both of quality and of innovation.

Without any doubt, an outstanding contribution was made by a dedicated amateur turned miniature book publisher, my late friend Achille J. St. Onge of Worcester, Massachusetts, USA, who was known as Archie to thousands of booklovers all over the world. With an uncanny instinct he chose texts which appealed and his standards of production were very high, reflecting his almost fanatical devotion to the world of minibibliophily. Many of his books, none of them of tiny size, were printed by renowned printers, such as the old-established firm of Enschedé en Zonen in Haarlem, Holland, he entrusted the binding of his volumes, clad in exquisite leathers, to great bookbinders such as Sangorski and Sutcliffe in London, and his limited editions are distinguished by the use of quality paper. Archie's publishing activities covered a long span of time, beginning with his first title **Noel, Christmas Echoes down the Ages** by Robert K. Shaw in 1935, right up to his death in April, 1978 at the premature age of 65. A checklist of his miniature volumes published in 1969 comprised 37 titles. The size of the volumes varied from $2\frac{1}{4}$ by $1\frac{1}{2}$ inches to $2\frac{15}{16}$ by $1\frac{7}{8}$ inches. They were bound in calf, niger morocco and other leathers of many different colours. In his frequently issued and widely distributed publicity handouts St. Onge always made a point of his "excellent miniature books making delightful and distinctive gifts".

Early in his career he began to publish the inaugural addresses of American Presidents beginning in 1943 with that of Thomas Jefferson and continuing with those of Franklin Delano Roosevelt, Eisenhower, John F. Kennedy, Lyndon Johnson and Richard Nixon. Being a great anglophile, St. Onge published in 1952 Winston Churchill's **King George the Sixth, the Prime**

Minister's broadcast, in 1953 **The Coronation Service of Her Majesty, Queen Elizabeth II,** in 1963 **Sir Winston Churchill, Honorary Citizen of the United States** and in 1965 **The Magna Carta of King John, A.D. 1215** for which he commissioned a special frontispiece using my good offices for that purpose.

The literary works, beginning with his second book **Friendship** by Emerson issued in 1939, include quotations from Thoreau, Gray's **Elegy, The Night before Christmas** by Clement C. Moore and **Shelley** by Swinburne. Other books of special interest are **Father of the Space Age** being the autobiography of Robert Hutchings Goddard, illustrated with photographic plates and using, very amusingly, an original U.S. postage stamp for a frontispiece. Archie improved on this unusual step by using for his **Historic American Flags** 10 actual USA stamps to illustrate his subject. That title was published in 1968, printed in 2000 copies on finest handmade paper by Enschedé and bound in blue niger morocco. At least two of the St. Onge

THE ADDRESSES OF HER MAJESTY QUEEN ELIZABETH II. Worcester, Massachusetts, Achille J. St. Onge, 1977. Title page and frontispiece.

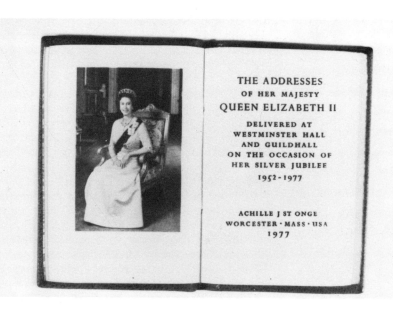

THE ADDRESSES
OF HER MAJESTY
QUEEN ELIZABETH II

DELIVERED AT
WESTMINSTER HALL
AND GUILDHALL
ON THE OCCASION OF
HER SILVER JUBILEE
1952-1977

ACHILLE J ST ONGE
WORCESTER · MASS · USA
1977

volumes are specifically concerned with the world of books. They are **Formats and Foibles** by Walter Hart Blumenthal and **The Remarks at the Dedication of the Wallace Library** by Archibald MacLeish, the great American librarian. Religious texts include **Sermon of his Eminence, Francis Cardinal Spellman, 1957, The Jewish Festivals** by Louis Jacobs and **The Twenty-Third Psalm,** illustrated by Tasha Tudor and published in 1965. One of his last creations marked again Achille St. Onge's great interest in British affairs. It was **The Addresses of Her Majesty Queen Elizabeth II, delivered at Westminster Hall and Guildhall on the Occasion of Her Silver Jubilee 1952-1977,** with a splendid coloured photograph portrait as frontispiece. We are quoting the entire colophon of this volume as a typical example of the care with which the Worcester Press planned its miniature books: "One thousand copies of this book were printed from Perpetua type on Crown & Sceptre paper at the Stanbrook Abbey Press, Worcester, England. Photograph by Peter Grugeon lithographed at Skelton's Press. Binding by Weatherby Woolnough was planned by Sydney M. Cockerell with drawings by Joan Tebbutt. He executed one special copy illuminated by Margaret Adams for presentation to Her Majesty the Queen".

Other recent miniature book publishers of quality in the United States include The Black Cat Press of Norman W. Forgue in Chicago and later at Skokie near that city which published amongst many other interesting literary, historical and even technical titles **Book Gluttons and Book Gourmets,** another of Walter Hart Blumenthal's original and fascinating titles, and The Hillside Press of Franklin, New Hampshire which later transferred to Buffalo in the state of New York. They published in strictly limited edition some works by Hans Christian Andersen, Holbein's Dance of Death, Nursery Rhymes, a Blake and other fine miniature books measuring circa $2\frac{3}{16}$ by $1\frac{13}{16}$ inches.

Dawson's Book Shop in Los Angeles is one of

the American Meccas for miniature book collectors. Many finely designed items were issued under their imprint, or that of Susan and Karen Dawson in Pasadena. Quite a few of these books are very small and all fall within our 3-inch limit. Associated with Dawson's and often working for them is Bela Blau of Los Angeles who is handsetting, printing and binding some delightful volumes. One of them, entitled **Up 65 Years to Larchmont** by Francis J. Weber tells the history of Dawson's in a smart little book bound in green leather, issued in 1970 and measuring $1\frac{9}{16}$ by $1\frac{3}{16}$ inches.

The Le Petit Oiseau Press in Chicago published miniature books designed, handset, printed and bound by Doris V. Welsh who is one of the great authorities on miniature books and worked as a librarian at the famous Newberry Library. Amongst the volumes she produced are **To a Skylark** by Shelley, issued in 1952, comprising 22 leaves, printed in 4-point Century Expanded type, measuring $1\frac{5}{8}$ by $2\frac{1}{4}$ inches and limited to 100 copies. Another example of her work is **Hurricane 1926. Reported by Garnet Varner Welsh and Earle Basil Welsh,** a very original book printed in 1958 in only 50 copies and measuring 2 by $1\frac{1}{2}$ inches.

The Schori Press in Evanston, Illinois, Barbara J. Raheb of Tarzana, California, Robert D. Naiva in Concord, New Hampshire, J. R. Levien, first of Enkhuizen, Holland and later publishing in New York under the imprint of The Traders Press, The Kittemaug Press of Spartanburg, South Carolina, The Mosaic Press in Cincinnati, The Ford Press of Hongkong and Lake Worth, Florida, Pall W. Bohne's Bookhaven Press in South San Gabriel, California, are only some of the considerable number of 20th century miniature book publishers active in the United States. Their products are varied and selected with circumspection. After a visit I received from the proprietor of the first-named press, Mr. Ward Schori, a dedicated minibook lover, I feel that his list is characteristic of the American scene and am therefore naming

172

some of the titles he published in recent years. Their sizes vary between $2\frac{3}{4}$ by $2\frac{1}{4}$ inches and $2\frac{1}{2}$ by $1\frac{7}{8}$ inches and one feature they all have in common is a detailed and informative colophon leaf, a laudable aid to bibliophily frequently encountered in U.S.A. miniature volumes. The smallest of Schori's books I have selected is **Lincoln, the Literary Genius** by Barzun, 49 pages, an existing book re-written and miniaturised by photolithography in 1977. Other titles are: **A Psalm of David,** by Ely E. Pilchik, finely bound in gilt-tooled leather by Bela Blau and published for a Los Angeles bookseller; **The Ballad of Yukon Jake** by Edward E. Paramore, Jr. with interesting illustrations and partly calligraphic text which is a parody of Robert W. Service's poems; a religious volume **A Stranger Passed** by G. H. Petty, issued in 1978; **Mark Twain on Horseback** by Caroline Thomas Harnsberger, with portrait and illustrations in "sanguine", bound by the Diez art bindery in Madrid, also dated 1978; a very unusual volume published in 1980 entitled **Came the Dawn. Guffaws from the Dumb Movies** by P. K. Thomajan, late of the Harold Lloyd Corporation and illustrated with a droll cartoon and stills from old movies.

Four American publishers who are all working at present need singling out because of the special talents they are bringing to the American miniature book field. The first is Robert E. Massmann, Director of Library Services at the Central Connecticut State College, New Britain, who has created miniature book curiosities of extraordinary character and originality, including his **Magic Nursery Rhymes** already mentioned in chapter twenty and **Consumer Rationing in World War Two,** 1979, in 2 volumes measuring an oblong $1\frac{1}{2}$ by 2 inches, where the second volume has a cover which is a reduced facsimile of a war ration book and contains genuine fuel and food ration stamps and Office of Price Administration tokens. Earlier Massmann publications include **Pearls from Kipling,** 1963, measuring $2\frac{1}{4}$ by 2 inches, **How the**

Art of Printing was Invented, 1964 and a miniature bookmark measuring $1\frac{7}{8}$ by $1\frac{1}{8}$ inches.

Of particular distinction and most attractive are some of the books published by Anne and David Bromer of Watertown, Massachusetts. Two of the finest are **The Butterfly's Ball and the Grasshopper's Feast,** reprinted from Roscoe's famous early 19th century children's book in a limited edition of 150 copies with 10 enchanting full-page wood-engravings, measuring $2\frac{3}{8}$ by 2 inches, and Emily Dickinson's **Poems of Life,** issued in 1977 in a limited edition of 125 copies, measuring $2\frac{3}{8}$ by $1\frac{5}{8}$ inches.

The Somesuch Press of Stanley Marcus, a retired magnate of the commercial world who founded the world-famous Neiman-Marcus store in Dallas, Texas, has been producing precious and unusual miniature volumes during the last few years. The first volume issued was a miniature edition of Marcus' book **Minding the Store. A Memoir,** limited to 500 numbered copies signed by the author, with portrait frontispiece, 32 full-page plates, XII and 384 pages and measuring $2\frac{15}{16}$ by $1\frac{15}{16}$ inches. **A Christmas Tree** by A. C. Greene, was hand-set in Centaur and Arrighi type, measuring $2\frac{7}{8}$ by $2\frac{1}{8}$ inches. One of the most prodigious efforts of the Somesuch Press is a deluxe miniature edition **Portraits of the Queen. The Stamp Collages of Jack Milroy,** printed in an edition of 100 copies at the Rara Avis Press in Madison, Wisconsin in 1979 and measuring $2\frac{7}{8}$ by $2\frac{5}{8}$ inches. It is of immense philatelic, artistic and royal interest and certainly unique in the miniature book field. The price is understandably high, $245.

Jane Bernier's Borrower's Press in Winterport, Maine has since 1974 produced what she herself in her prospectus calls "micro miniature books that are also beautiful private press books". She continues: "Only the finest materials are used: paper milled to .0025 inches for the text, fine skiver leather and linen cloth in a variety of colors, and fine handmade marbled papers for bindings ... Most books are illustrated and most are me-

ticulously colored by hand ... All books are printed
entirely by hand on a small letterpress ... hand-
sewn and handbound". Amongst the splendid tiny
volumes are **Star Signs. Twelve Zodiac Signs,**
32 pages, $\frac{3}{4}$ by $\frac{1}{2}$ of an inch, 1977; **Wildflowers**
with 18 delightful coloured etchings of flowers by
Jane Conneen, 1 by $\frac{7}{8}$ inches, 1977; **Blake's
Poetry,** $\frac{7}{8}$ by $\frac{5}{8}$ of an inch, 1978; **Adventure of the
Veiled Lodger** by Conan Doyle, 80 pages, $\frac{7}{8}$ by $\frac{5}{8}$
of an inch, 1978, and **Aesop's Fables** with hand-
coloured illustrations, $\frac{7}{8}$ by $\frac{5}{8}$ of an inch, also 1978.
A particularly appropriate and charming miniature
volume is **Puppet Theatre: The Art** by Coad
Canada Puppets with coloured frontispiece and
black-and-white illustrations, 80 pages, $\frac{3}{4}$ by $\frac{5}{8}$ of an
inch, 1980. **A Visit from St. Nicholas** by Clement
Clarke Moore also appeared in 1980, with six
enchanting hand-coloured illustrations, 29 pages,
bound in crimson leather and measuring $\frac{3}{4}$ by $\frac{5}{8}$ of
an inch. It is limited to 350 numbered and signed
copies. Earlier titles which went very quickly out of
print are **Cinderella, Herb Cookery, Little Red
Ridinghood, Love Sonnets** and others. Jane
Bernier has to our knowledge produced the most
consistent list of really tiny books, all under one
inch high, in the entire history of miniature book
production and her volumes are almost without
exception beautiful and ideal for dolls' house
libraries, etc. Much skill, patience and above all
devotion must have gone into their manufacture.

In Europe, by far the greatest production of
miniature books has taken and is still taking place
in Hungary where during the years 1948 to 1975
alone 462 volumes were published, which are all
listed in the fine multi-lingual bibliography compiled by Gyula Janka, Hungary's foremost
producer and collector of miniature books.

It is of course impossible to mention them all
and it would be invidious to pick out a few. It must
however be stated quite emphatically that in the
quality of printing, the beauty of layout and design,
the unendingly varied creation of splendid bindings
and the interest of many of the texts they leave

collectively, and as a national effort, most other European miniature books of our time far behind. This may be partly due to the fact that in a communist country there undoubtedly exists tighter central control of literary output and that the comparative shortage of industrial and domestic consumer goods has made the collecting of miniature books one of the few outlets for the acquisitive instinct and the collector's urge. But there can be no doubt at all about the very real talent, inventiveness and high artistic ability lavished on these splendid minibooks.

Many volumes contain, as may be expected, political texts, especially by Marx, Engels, Lenin and Hungarian communist leaders, also a fascinating volume printing the "International" song in 55 different languages and many different scripts. Quite a few literary texts are also available including Petöfi, the great native poet, Baudelaire, Schiller, Rabindranath Tagore, Pablo Neruda and others. Of particular interest are fine facsimile reprints of famous first editions like that of Copernicus' **De revolutionibus orbium coelestium** of 1543 or of the musical score of Bela Bartok's **Quartetto One, op. 7.** A finely decorated

A collection of modern Hungarian miniature books (Reduced size).

176

volume reproduces initials of the sixteenth to eighteenth century used in books of the Egyetemi Nyomda publishing house in Budapest. Several tiny volumes contain excellent colour reproductions of Hungarian and foreign paintings of past and present times or illustrate fine architecture, porcelain or costume. A well-documented work deals with space exploration, another shows the Hungarian stamps issued under the present régime a luxury edition of which contains samples of actual postage stamps. Another miniature volume is distinguished by finely illuminated illustrations in gold and colour of Hungarian city arms and a number of enchanting books depict Hungarian and foreign historic towns in expressive woodcuts by the artist Károly Andruskó. Two attractive tomes, **Variaciok** and **Pastorale** are graced by the beautiful and often quite erotic illustations of Károly Reich. We have already referred to Gyula Janka's bibliographies of Hungarian miniature books. The same author has also written and published a number of other volumes devoted to the collecting of miniature books which we have listed in the bibliography at the end of this volume.

Many of the Hungarian miniature books have texts in several languages, chiefly English, Russian, German and French in addition to the Hungarian. The sizes vary from $\frac{7}{8}$ by $\frac{11}{16}$ of an inch to $2\frac{3}{4}$ by 2 inches. Quite a few were issued in large numbers up to about 8000 copies, especially the political texts, while other editions are strictly limited to a few hundred or even occasionally to 40 or less copies. Their circulation is frequently restricted to members of miniature book clubs or circles and they are therefore not obtainable in shops. While most bindings are in cloth or imitation leather, some are in fine moroccos or calf. But whatever their material, they are all of splendid appearance, decorated in gilt or silver, often with illustrations on the covers, and in a number of cases with dustjackets. For protection the publishers issue their tiny volumes frequently in perspex cases or give them transparent cellophane jackets. They are invariably printed on high-class paper, often on artpaper. The colophon pages give credit to the various artists, designers and craftsmen involved in the production of the volumes.

A fair number of miniature books have been produced and are still being issued in the German Democratic Republic. The most ambitious one is perhaps a ten-volume set of Boccaccio's **Das Dekameron,** published by Zentrag in Berlin 1972/3, with illustrations by Werner Klemke, measuring $2\frac{3}{16}$ by $1\frac{9}{16}$ inches. Goethe's **Faust** was produced on the occasion of the Leipzig "Buchkunst-Ausstellung", exhibition of book art, in 1965, comprising 685 pages, size $1\frac{7}{8}$ by $1\frac{1}{2}$ inches. Amongst a large number of political texts, the publication of Rosa Luxemburg's **Briefe aus dem Zuchthaus,** (Letters from Prison), deserves special mention. It was brought out by the Dietz Verlag in Berlin in 1971, has 347 pages and measures $1\frac{7}{8}$ by $1\frac{1}{2}$ inches. Other East European countries including the Soviet Union, Czechoslovakia, Yugoslavia, Poland and Roumania are also producing miniature books but none of them on the scale or of the quality of the best of the Hungarian output.

In Italy, Leopardi's **Dialoghi** was published by the Libreria del Teatro in Florence in 1943, in the middle of World War Two. Printed by Artigianelli it has 84 pages, measures only $\frac{3}{4}$ by $\frac{1}{2}$ of an inch and was well produced by process of photographic reduction. The colophon speaks of a limitation to 250 copies but we have seen so many copies that this does not appear very credible.

A Spanish miniature book which used to be encountered quite frequently but has now become scarce is the 2-volume edition of **El Ingenioso Hidalgo Don Quijote de la Mancha** by Cervantes, published in 1947 and at later dates by Ediciones Castilla in Madrid, measuring $2\frac{7}{16}$ by $1\frac{13}{16}$ inches. The book is produced by photolithography, printed on very thin paper and bound in gilt-stamped green leather. **Os Lusiadas,** the great work by Luiz de Camoens, was published in its original Portuguese by Schmidt & Günther in

Leipzig circa 1930, measuring $2\frac{1}{2}$ by 2 inches. Da Costa in Lisbon brought out a facsimile of the first edition of that work (Lisbon, 1572) in 1954, measuring $3\frac{1}{2}$ by $2\frac{5}{16}$ inches. A Mexican miniature book, **Testamento del Pensador Mexicano** was published by G. M. Echaniz in Mexico City in 1963. Its author is José Joaquin Fernandez de Lizardi, it measures $2\frac{3}{8}$ by $1\frac{3}{4}$ inches, comprises 66 pages and is bound in pale mottled leather richly stamped in gilt. 300 copies were specially printed in 6-point type on Ameca Bond paper for Dawson's of Los Angeles, an interesting miniature book collaboration between two countries. Other Spanish-language miniatures, but of fairly poor quality are the illustrated booklets for children, published with coloured wrappers by S. Calleja in Madrid over many years, measuring $2\frac{3}{4}$ by 2 inches.

Some tiny volumes were also printed in the Catalan language which is spoken in the region around Barcelona, Spain. An interesting earlier venture was the "Biblioteca Minúscula Catalana" edited by Eugenia Simon and finely printed from small type. Volume I is **La Patria** by the great Catalan writer Carlos Arribau i Farriols, published in Barcelona in 1921, comprising 112 pages and Volume II is **La Vida de Santa Eulalia Verge,** 1922, of 42 pages; both books measure $1\frac{9}{16}$ by $1\frac{1}{8}$ inches. 100 copies were printed on ordinary paper, 20 on seventeenth century paper and another 20 on Japanese vellum.

A considerable number of very small and unpretentious miniature volumes were published by André Kundig in Geneva, printed nicely in monotype 5-point New Times Roman and measuring $1\frac{1}{2}$ by $1\frac{1}{8}$ inches. Amongst the titles are **Pensées Chinoises,** 1954, **Proverbes Bantous,** 1956, **Pensées Anglaises,** 1962, **Pensées Médiévales,** 1970, and many other similar titles. Most of them have just under 100 pages and are bound in stiff wrappers of different colours. Notwithstanding their modest appearance and price these little books are true miniatures created with care and textually valuable. The "Diogenes Mini-Taschenbücher" on the other hand, published in Zürich since the early

1970's, although technically miniature books measuring $2\frac{13}{16}$ by $1\frac{3}{4}$ inches, are really ordinary paperbacks of modern and classical literature, chiefly in translations. They use much of the available page space to advertise larger-sized volumes and can only marginally fit into a collector's library.

In Britain not many miniature books are being produced at the present time. We have already mentioned the Gleniffer Press in Paisley, Scotland. One of their more interesting books is **Betjeman in Miniature** containing selected poems by Sir John Betjeman, the Poet Laureate. It was published in 1976 in 250 copies with 24 leaves and measuring $1\frac{7}{8}$ by $1\frac{1}{2}$ inches. Fairly recently, F. C. Avis of London issued **The Lilliputian Ode** by Alexander Pope, an attractively printed volume of 21 pages, bound in flexible leather and measuring $1\frac{7}{8}$ by $1\frac{1}{2}$ inches. A well-produced and attractive English miniature book **Little Things to Please Little Minds** was published in 1979 by the Rampant Lion Press in Cambridge, limited to 400 copies and illustrated in black-and-white by James Bruce. Bound in marbled boards, it has only 12 leaves and measures $2\frac{3}{16}$ by $1\frac{1}{4}$ inches.

The Black Sun Press in Paris published in July 1929 **The Sun** by Harry Crosby with drawings by Caresse Crosby. Printed in 100 copies on Japan paper by François Bret in Roman Corps 3 from the fount of Deberny & Peignot, it measures only 1 by $\frac{3}{4}$ inches. The same press produced in 1930 a **Rubaiyat of Omar Khayyam** in an edition of 44 copies measuring $1\frac{3}{16}$ by $1\frac{1}{4}$ inches. As may be imagined both these volumes are extremely rare.

Amongst twentieth century Scandinavian miniature books, we would like to mention Esaias Tegnér's **Fritiofs Saga,** illustrated by Knut Ekwall and published by Allhems Tryckerier in Malmö, Sweden in 1959. The finely produced volume was bound in gilt-stamped sheepskin, measures $2\frac{1}{8}$ by $1\frac{7}{16}$ inches and comprises 146 pages: Xavier de Maistre's **Rejse i mit Kamer,** translated from the French into Danish by Else

Schäffer Wolf with fine tinted illustrations by Ebbe Sadolin was published in Copenhagen by Grafisk Cirkel in 1943, during the German occupation of Denmark. This translation of the famous **Voyage autour de ma chambre** has 190 pages, is limited to 100 numbered copies and measures $2\frac{1}{8}$ by $1\frac{7}{8}$ inches. It is not surprising that the work of Denmark's most widely known author, Hans Christian Andersen, has found its way into the world of tiny books. **Fire Eventir. Vanddraaben. De Smaa Gronne. Den Onde Fyrste Laserne,** an illustrated edition, was publihed in 1943 at Haderslev by K. E. Wulff, size $1\frac{13}{16}$ by $1\frac{1}{2}$ inches. **Den lille Pige med Svovlstikkerne** with Andersen's portrait and 4 illustrations was issued by Harlang & Toskvig in Copenhagen in the 1950's, measuring $1\frac{15}{16}$ by $1\frac{1}{4}$ inches. A Swedish miniature volume on the **Codex Argenteus** measuring $1\frac{1}{4}$ by 1 inches was published in Uppsala in 1959, containing information on that famous document in Swedish, English, French and German. It is contained in a silver box of $1\frac{3}{8}$ by $1\frac{1}{8}$ inches reproducing a celebrated 17th century silver binding.

Amongst earlier Scandinavian books we have seen are **Aegteskabs-Katechismus** (A Marriage Catechism), containing poems which was produced circa 1860 by Groebes Bogtrykkeri in Copenhagen, measuring $1\frac{3}{4}$ by $1\frac{1}{2}$ inches and various issues of a **Fick-Kalender** measuring about 2 by $1\frac{1}{2}$ inches, the 1874 issue printed on pink paper and published by P. A. Norstedt in Stockholm while the 1882 edition was issued by the Kongl. Boktrykkeriet in the same city, containing details of the Swedish Royal family.

At the present moment one of the most fertile countries in the field of minibook production is Japan, where the collecting habit is making great strides and the production of such volumes is by no means confined to the record-breaking "smallest books in the world" to which we have already referred earlier. It is beyond the scope of this book to draw a detailed picture of the Japanese scene but we would like to draw attention to catalogue No.

375 published by Dawson's Book Shop in Los Angeles which under the title "Mame-Hon. Miniature Books from Japan" lists over 200 such items of which the proprietors of that firm have specialised knowledge dating back to a prolonged stay in Japan. During recent years we have however been privileged to see and possess some of the very charming profusely illustrated miniature volumes originating in that country and find them well worthy of mention.

Quite a few of them are the work of Yonejiro Sato, an outstanding woodcut artist who teaches at Aomori College in Aomori City. All were produced in small editions numbering often only 50 copies. Several volumes consist of beautifully designed coloured woodcuts of bookplates, affixed to a folding strip of the finest Japanese paper and bound in flexible boards decorated with one of the woodcuts contained therein. They measure $1\frac{7}{8}$ by $1\frac{7}{16}$ inches and are preserved in plastic boxes with decorated transparent lids. Other volumes due to the same artist are **Tsugaru Hogen Gacho,** Japanese local dialect picture, and **Tsugaru-Kotoba,** Japanese local language, with 14 and 15 expressive coloured woodcuts respectively measuring $1\frac{7}{16}$ by $1\frac{7}{8}$ inches, printed about 1970, and like the previous items in flexible boards in Japanese style. Further volumes illustrated and printed by Sato are **Biographical Writings about Christ** consisting of 17 pages with woodcut text and illustrations, measuring $1\frac{1}{4}$ by $1\frac{1}{4}$ inches which were limited to 200 copies, bound in wine-coloured velvet and preserved in attractive wooden boxes with titling label, and **The Story of Asamushi Spa** with 14 gaily coloured woodcuts, of the same size and the same restricted number of copies as the previous item.

Two very small volumes published in Tokyo in the late 1960's are **Yabu-no-naka** and **To-shi-shun,** both written by Akutagawa and containing 128 and 132 pages. They measure $\frac{7}{8}$ by $\frac{11}{16}$ of an inch and are bound in blue boards with vignettes on both covers, and in plain olive boards respectively, both preserved in yellow cardboard slipcases. The first item is printed in black and red and both have portrait frontispieces. At about the same time an edition of **Aesop's Fables** appeared in Tokyo, comprising 72 pages, measuring 1 by $\frac{3}{4}$ inches and enhanced by coloured illustrations which are a curious mixture of a traditional Japanese style and of pop art. Another very small volume we have seen is a collection of Japanese poems by Takuboku with a portrait, also published in the Japanese capital during the 1960's, bound in lilac boards with a red cardboard slipcase and measuring $\frac{7}{8}$ by $\frac{5}{8}$ of an inch.

Besides some lovely children's books on folding strips containing 3 double-page and 30 half-page coloured pictures measuring an oblong $1\frac{3}{4}$ by $2\frac{9}{16}$ inches, we have also seen a book containing the **Inauguration Speech by President Jimmy Carter** published in January 1978 by Bijou Book Hoshino in Tokyo in a limited numbered edition of 150 copies, comprising 96 pages and measuring 1 by $\frac{15}{16}$ inches. A curious feature of this book bound in dark-brown niger morocco is the fact that the number given to the copy is shown on an 18 carat gold panel laid into the upper cover, while President Carter's initials "J.C." are stamped on that cover in platinum leaf. It must however be said that this lavishing of precious metals has failed to create a particularly beautiful miniature volume, although the printing of the text in English and Japanese is superbly clear.

A recent Japanese miniature item is the **Hun-Nya Shingyo,** one of the most popular Buddhist prayers in Japan which was published in Tokyo in January 1980 and consists of a scroll in Chinese and Sanskrit characters with three illustrations, enclosed in a special hand-made wooden case. The scroll measures 2 by 32 inches, is printed on the famous Japanese Torinoko paper and when rolled up is covered by a Kawashima silk weave. The Addo-Rie Studio was responsible for the elaborate manufacture of this item, limited to 100 numbered copies and characteristic of the care and attention

183

which so frequently has been concentrated on miniature books in many lands.

This chapter devoted to present developments will have convinced our readers of the abiding vitality of this field of bibliophily. The dedicated producers of miniature books, especially in the United States of America, Hungary and Japan, are assuring our hobby of a brilliant future. I do not hesitate to predict that future generations will carry on the tradition established by today's collectors who are the subject of our last chapter.

Some of the modern miniature books published by J. R. Levien, at Enkhuizen, Holland, ca. 1970.

All books shown one-half size

COLLECTORS
AND
COLLECTIONS

With such an abundance of material available it is not surprising that miniature books have become, at least during the last hundred or so years, the eagerly sought after objects of many specialised collections. Amongst the earliest well-documented ones is that of Alfred Brockhaus in Leipzig, a member of the notable German publishing family whose library of microscopic prints and formats comprised 98 volumes. When Arnold Kuczynski published a list of that collection in 1888, he conveyed in his preface the owner's desire and hope that the very existence of the catalogue might encourage people to offer him further miniature volumes for his approval. Many items in the Brockhaus collection exceeded by far our 3-inch limit but it included such tiny rarities as Krylof's **Fables** of 1837, Salmin's **Dantino,** and **Quads within Quads** as well as some very elusive 17th century German devotional works.

The widely famed library of Monsieur Georges Salomon in Paris also found a bibliographer in the person of Gaston Tissandier, who, in 1894, recorded its treasures in a summary account, in which he called it with full justification, "the biggest library of the smallest books in the world". When visiting Salomon he was astounded to behold these "microbes of the book world which numbered about seven hundred French and foreign volumes, ranging from the most frivolous to the most severe". The largest of these books measured $2\frac{1}{8}$ by $1\frac{1}{4}$ inches. The most interesting part of the collection included many very small French, German and English almanacs in delightful bindings. It also included the **Charte Constitutionelle** of 1792, **Des Alten und Neuen Testaments Mittler** illustrated by the Küsell sisters, a 17th century German devotional work entitled **Vom Christlichen Hausstand,** (Of the Christian Household), published in Nuremberg in 1666, and other noteworthy rarities. A large part of that library eventually found its way into the collection of Arthur A. Houghton, Jr. to which we refer below.

Charles Elton (1839-1900), a lawyer and antiquary, together with Mary Elton assembled an important collection of miniature books which was sold at Sotheby's auction rooms in London on May 1st, 1916. A short essay by the Elton's entitled "Little Books" was first published in 1900 and reprinted by the Ford Press at Lake Worth, Florida, in 1977.

Wilbur Macey Stone, one of the most prominent American collectors of tiny books, has been called the "dean of microbibliophiles" because of his intense involvement in that field. He lived in East Orange, New Jersey, where he not only assembled a very fine collection but used his knowledge to promote the love of miniature books through his scholarly publications on Taylor's Thumb Bibles, Boreman's Gigantick Histories and other prominent ventures in the field. Stone described how he became a collector starting from his love of early children's books. "The virus of the desire to collect miniature books spread in my bookish veins and I became a hopeless case, to my great satisfaction and joy." His collection started with the children's books illustrated by Alfred Mills, proceeded to include many rare and beautiful 18th and 19th century almanacs and he later concentrated on miniature thumb Bibles which became his great love and on which he became a great expert.

Stone also became the main driving force in bringing together the Club of the LXIVmos, a loose grouping of American miniature book lovers which published at irregular intervals the famous *Newsletter of the LXIVmos* under the devoted editorship of James D. Henderson. Under the self-styled title "the Scrivener", Henderson presided very ably over the publication of twenty-one issues, mainly from Brookline in the state of Massachusetts. Some issues were however farmed out to other places for editing and printing thus deliberately spreading the collecting habit. Thus special numbers of the *Newsletter* appeared in Leipzig, Chicago and Amsterdam under the sponsorship of local bibliophiles like Dr. Säuberlich,

186

Douglas C. McMurtrie and Menno Hertzberger. Henderson himself became an ardent collector, followed in that field many years later by his son.

Franklin Delano Roosevelt, the great American President, also became a collector of miniature books. In May 1929 he wrote to Henderson: "My own tiny books are neither very rare nor very numerous but I continue my interest in them". He possessed 162 items, most of them under 3 inches high and none of them exceeding 4 inches. As late as April 1973, the Swann Auction Galleries in New York sold some Pickering Diamond Classics, namely the Milton, the Cicero, the Petrarch and the Catullus which were inscribed on the flyeaf by Roosevelt.

One of the most meticulous and successful collectors of miniature books was Miss Vera von Rosenberg, the daughter of a Russian Imperial Councillor whose passion for such items started when still a child, after a friend had presented her with some of these tiny treasures. The contents of her library were listed with great care in 1929 by Robert W. Petri in **Mikrobiblion.** It describes in detail her 379 volumes from which she excluded all almanacs, but which contained some of the finest miniature books ever printed, including fourteen dating back to the 16th century, 35 from the 17th century, 34 18th century volumes and 82 important 19th century books. The collection also contained a few early manuscripts, and a number of volumes exceeding our 3-inch limit. As early as October 1928, the Rosenberg miniatures were offered for sale by G. Hess in Munich who took out a full-page advertisement in the *Newsletter of the LXIVmos* No. 11 mentioning "380 miniature books XVIth to XIXth cent." We do not know if the Bavarian firm was successful in disposing of the collection. We do know, however, that a large portion of the library was sold by Sotheby's in London on the 22nd of July 1974, listed as the property of G. J. Sassoon, Esq., including not only many very fine books but also all the bibliographical material, index cards and manuscript notes brought together for the

187

cataloguing of the Rosenberg volumes in the **Mikrobiblion** publication.

Her Majesty Queen Mary, who cherished her world-famous dolls' house, also took a great interest in the books it contains. They are described in considerable detail in **The Book of the Queen's Dolls' House Library** edited by E. V. Lucas and published by Methuen in London in 1924. The library contains many volumes specially written by hand by famous authors. Amongst the printed books is a very beautiful and precious volume, **Carmina Sapphica** by Horatius Flaccus, printed by the Ashendene Press in 1923 and measuring only $1\frac{3}{8}$ by 1 inches. As Lucas in his preface to **The Book of the Queen's Dolls' House Library** writes, it was set up by St. John Hornby "for his own pleasure and photographed down for ours". A presentation copy of that volume from the printer to Sir Sidney Cockerell was sold at auction in 1956. Other printed books owned by Queen Mary include **The Mite,** 1891, donated by its publisher E. A. Robinson, the tiny Bradshaw and Railway ABC already mentioned by us, Schloss's English Bijou Almanacs from 1836 to 1842, various early children's bibles, the tiniest volumes published by Bryce, **Small Rain upon the Tender Herb,** the Christmas Stories of Charles Dickens, the miniature atlas specially created for the occasion, the "Ellen Terry" Shakespeare set, a few of the charming illustrated volumes published by Pairault in Paris and some of the attractive French miniature almanacs of the early 1800's.

Thomas Warburton of Manchester not only published articles on miniature books, but I know that he had also assembled a large collection including many rarities. Unfortunately I was never able to obtain any details, but I had the opportunity, or should I rather say back luck, to see many of his miniature books carried around by a gentleman who had apparently inherited them after Warburton's death. They were loosely thrown together in a large suitcase, without any protection and many of the items, which I had only a few minutes to examine, were of extraordinary beauty and outstanding scarcity. In my early collecting days I had frequently corresponded with Mr. Warburton about various miniature book problems and was always amazed by his insight and helpfulness.

Dr. Percy E. Spielmann, a noted chemist and road expert, came late in life to his hobby of collecting miniature books although he had grown up in a bookish tradition as the son of M. H. Spielmann, a well-known author on bibliophile subjects. Percy was well into his seventies when he decided to build up his collection, but once started on that road he never looked back. Miniature books did not become an obsession with him, but collecting them turned itself into a way of life, and provided him with constant delight. In 1961 his **Catalogue of the Library of Miniature Books collected by Percy E. Spielmann** saw the light of day under the imprint of Edward Arnold in London. He included in that volume what he called "descriptive summaries" which were entirely his own work and will demonstrate to the most casual reader the liveliness of his interest and the acuity of his mind. The actual bibliographical entries he entrusted to me as I knew all his books intimately. He kept his library in beautiful condition, and arranged it with great taste and love. It contained many very rare volumes and was in any case a splendid mirror of the riches of this lilliputian world of letters. When he died in 1964 at the age of 83, he left behind a library comprising 848 volumes, contained in eight small bookcases, including one covered with red morocco and lettered "Temple of the Muses". Not long after his death, "the well known collection of miniature books formed by the late Dr. Percy E. Spielmann" was sold by Sotheby's at their book auction of the 21st July 1964 in one single lot thus making its survival as an integrated whole much more likely. The collection was indeed bought not by a dealer, who would have dispersed it, but by Julian I. Edison of St. Louis, Missouri, U.S.A. who added it to his collection and has continued to build it up ever since. In 1965 it numbered already over 2200 tomes.

Edison, like a few other major collectors before him, has earned the gratitude of miniature book lovers by imparting his extensive knowledge acquired in the purchase of these books to the entire bibliophile community through his *Miniature Book News* published since 1965. These slender but copiously illustrated and carefully researched news-sheets have remained one of the major sources of information existing in the field and have undoubtedly served as an inspiration to collectors and publishers of miniature books.

In December 1965, the Rare Book Department of the John M. Olin Library, Washington University at St. Louis staged an exhibition of miniature books from the Edison collection which was thus given its first public showing. Together with a beautifully produced catalogue containing an interesting introductory history of miniature books written by Edison himself, this venture served the valuable purpose of widening the circle of those who love these tiny masterpieces and gaining new friends for this bibliophile territory amongst the experts.

Throughout this book we have had occasion to refer to the collection assembled by Arthur A. Houghton, Junior who had been a major collector of rare books for many years. Although his miniature book library was only one of the sidelines of his collecting interests, it nevertheless grew into one of the finest ever assembled. When it came up for sale at Christie's auction in London on the 5th December 1979, it could truthfully be described in the preface to the finely produced catalogue as "the most important and the most comprehensive assembly of these tiny volumes ever offered for sale". Amongst the highlights were some magnificently illuminated miniature manuscripts of the fifteenth century, a few splendid books of hours of the early sixteenth century and an almost unparalleled collection of beautifully bound and illustrated almanacs from France, England, Italy, Austria and the Low Countries. Also included were Martin Parker's **An abstract of the historie of the renouned maiden Queene Elizabeth,** published in 1631 and George Peele's **The Tale of Troy,** 1604, both volumes the only recorded copies of these important early English miniature books. The Houghton collection has now been dispersed, but it was gratifying to note at the sale that many of the finest volumes went to owners of existing libraries, especially that of Julian I. Edison.

Amongst other notable collectors in the United States are Ruth E. Adomeit, Robert W. Bloch, Frances Dunn, Stanley Marcus, Doris V. Welsh and Julia P. Wightman.

Ruth Adomeit of Cleveland, Ohio, has a very large and important collection of miniature books. She has been particularly interested in thumb Bibles and has written a detailed and full bibliography of them, but her library of many thousand volumes transcends that comparatively narrow subject. Preceding Edison by five years, she started a quarterly publication, *The Miniature Book Collector* in June 1960 and it continued to appear until March 1962 when it had to close down as it was losing money. This excellent tiny periodical, measuring circa 4 by $3\frac{1}{2}$ inches, was published by St. Onge in Worcester, Massachusetts and contains much valuable information, made more accessible through the subsequent publication of an index volume.

Miss Adomeit's collection was exhibited with great success at the Cleveland Public Library in 1972.

Robert W. Bloch who runs a public relations firm in New York, started collecting about 1969. He has about 350 volumes which include many rare London Almanacks of the 18th century of which he is fond. His very special concern is with miniature book sets and more particularly with travelling libraries of which he owns the two most significant ones, the famous "Jones Portable Travelling Library" and the even rarer "Bibliothèque Portative du Voyageur".

191

Frances Dunn is a miniature book collector of long standing. She started collecting in 1931. As the Director of the Children's Division of the Public Libraries in Saginaw, Michigan, she established world-wide connections with other librarians and bibliophiles. Her most eminent possession is John Taylor, the Water Poet's, **Verbum Sempiternum** of 1614, the excessively rare first edition of that prototype of all thumb Bibles where the title is misspelled **Verbum Sempiternae.** The only other copy listed in the Short Title Catalogue No. 23810, is an imperfect one owned by the Aberdeen University Library. Frances Dunn's fine collection includes many other rarities and numbers over one thousand volumes.

We have already referred to Stanley Marcus of Dallas, Texas, as an important publisher of small books. Before his retirement from the world of big commerce, he was Chairman and Chief Executive of the world-famous store group of Neiman-Marcus in Dallas which has the reputation that you can order absolutely everything there, even a live elephant. There seems to be only a short step from the largest animal to the smallest books. Marcus' comprehensive collection of miniature books which he has selected with great scholarship, has achieved the supreme honour of being the object of an exhibition running from March to May 1978 at the Library of Congress, the national library of the United States located at Washington. Under the title "Miniature Book Collecting" it exhibited 115 carefully chosen volumes covering a wide field of interests from fine modern books to rare manuscripts and included some of the peaks of the art of the printer like Didot's **La Rochefoucauld** and Jannon's **Psalmes de David** of 1631. In a valuable introduction to the official catalogue Stanley Marcus wrote: "As a student of typography and bookmaking, I was fascinated with the variety of subject matter printed in miniature, by the skill of the various craftsmen, from printing to binding, and by the fact that almost every printer at one time or another felt impelled to produce a volume in miniature. Like all other fields of collecting, once you begin to learn more about the subject you become as firmly hooked as a fish which has swallowed the sinker".

Doris V. Welsh, an expert librarian who worked for many years at the renowned Newberry Library in Chicago and who has already been mentioned as a producer of fine miniature books at her private press, has been a collector for many years. She has also prepared a major bibliography of miniature books which we hope will eventually see the light of day and constitute a kind of "Brunet" or "Lowndes", as a standard work in the field.

Julia P. Wightman of New York has a fine collection of long standing, having concentrated on the rarest and most exquisite miniature books which became available to her. The **Short Title Catalogue of Books printed in England, Scotland and Ireland 1475-1640** tells us that she possesses one of the two only known copies of the seminal miniature book **An Agnus Dei,** (Lamb of God), by John Weever, in its first edition published in London in 1601, listed in the S.T.C. under No. 25220. Measuring $1\frac{1}{2}$ by 1 inches, that volume can be described as the first true miniature volume published in England. A copy of the third edition dated 1606, which *The Times* wrongly hailed as the "earliest recorded miniature book printed in England", fetched £1,250 at a book auction by Sotheby's on the 12th December, 1980.

Monsignor Francis J. Weber of Los Angles, California, briefly describes his collection of 575 titles in **Minibibliophilia,** a small volume measuring $2\frac{13}{16}$ by $2\frac{1}{8}$ inches, published in 1979 by Dawson's in Los Angeles. It includes many rare modern American items, a strong gathering of volumes published by Bryce in Glasgow and its oldest book is a copy of Meibom's **De Flagrorum Usu in re Veneria,** London, 1770.

There exist, of course, many other fine miniature book collections in the United States. We have chosen to confine ourselves to those which are well documented through bibliographies, exhibition ca-

193

talogues or specialised periodicals, but we know of ardent collectors in many different cities, towns and villages throughout North America, including Canada.

In Europe, the most widely known miniature book collection is that owned by Irene M. Winterstein of Zürich, Switzerland, who has been gathering it for over thirty years. In 1972 it already numbered 5,000 volumes and many more have been added since that date. The library is carefully arranged and fully catalogued in different categories ranging from almanacs and children's books to classical texts, Bibles, etc. Irene M. Winterstein's collection also includes a very special and beautiful assembly of the delightful *carnets de bal,* so popular during the last century. The many hundreds of tiny and beautiful almanacs include considerable rarities which are often unrecorded. The same applies to some of her children's books and classics. I have before me a colour photograph of the collection which looks dazzling and is greatly enhanced by the many finely carved and delicately designed special bookcases in which it is housed.

In Hungary where new miniature books make their appearance almost daily the collecting habit is not surprisingly very strongly developed. The best-known collection is without any doubt that of Gyula Janka, Secretary of the "Collectors of Miniature Books Club" of the University Press in Budapest, and Director of its printing house. He started his collection early in life, when he was given copies of Goethe's **Faust** and Schiller's **Maria Stuart,** two volumes published in Leipzig at the beginning of this century as part of the attractive "Lilliput-Bibliothek". Since then he has never looked back. In 1959 he had 93 miniature books and by 1974 he owned 2,680 volumes originating from 27 countries. A miniature book written by Gyula Kardos and published in Budapest in 1974 under the title **The Nestor of Collectors of Miniature Books** gives much information on Janka's collecting habits and mentions the many hundreds of letters he wrote to many

194

countries in the pursuit of his hobby. In addition, he has written many articles and given many lectures with the aim of popularising the collecting of tiny books. He also initiated a publication entitled *Mikrobibliofilok*, (Microbibliophiles), which has appeared at three-monthly intervals ever since January 1971 and of which he is the editor-in-chief. It is characteristic of the strength of miniature book collecting in Hungary and an indication of its steady growth that this specialised journal, with a circulation necessarily limited by the fact that not many outside Hungary can read the language, was initially printed in 300 copies, then in 800 and finally in 1,000 copies, which are supplied free to Hungarian miniature book clubs as well as to similar clubs abroad, notably the "Club of Fans of Miniature Books" in Moscow.

Japan has lately shown great interest in miniature books and several collectors have started libraries of tiny volumes. One of the more notable collectors is Kazushige Onuma, President of Periodica Japonica, Inc. in Tokyo, and organiser of the "Miniature Book Oval Saloon Lilliput". Another collector, Kazutoshi Sakamoto, was instrumental in organising a magnificent exhibition of miniature books in Tokyo. We now hear that Dr. Osagawara has started a Miniature Book Museum, surely the first in the world, at Fujieda near Tokyo, containing an extensive collection of what the Japanese call *Mame-Hon*, (Bean-sized Books).

Amongst the European libraries best known for their collections of miniature books are the British Library in London and the Bodleian Library in Oxford. Thanks to the courtesy of the Curator's staff, we recently had the opportunity of examining in detail the collection which the British Library has assembled in three miniature book cases stored, perhaps regrettably, in a glass case situated in a corridor behind the North Library which is rarely visited by the general public. The about 250 volumes in these cases do not include the fine collection of miniature bindings of **London Almanacks,** kept in a different place and which is

195

still being built up by the Librarian. They include however such rarities as the third edition of John Taylor's **Verbum Sempiternum,** with amendments, printed for Thomas James in London in 1693, another edition of the same text, printed and sold by Tho. Ilive in London at the Printing Press in Aldersgate in 1720, measuring $2\frac{3}{8}$ by 2 inches, the Virgil printed by Jannon in Sedan in 1625, the rare set of Spanish classics printed by Ginesta in Madrid between 1873 and 1875 which we have mentioned earlier, and many other unusual books. A masonic curiosity is **Pocket Booklet of the Royal Masonic Institution for Girls, being an Epitome of its History, together with general information,** St. John's Hill, Battersea Rise, London S.W. This booklet of 32 pages was published in London at Freemason's Hall in 1893 and measures $2\frac{3}{8}$ by $1\frac{5}{8}$ inches. Much less rare but nevertheless difficult to find are the many small volumes in original black wrappers published by T. Goode in London during the second half of the nineteenth century. Chiefly but by no means exclusively intended for young people, they include titles such as **The Lost Soul** (a poem), **A Dialogue between a King and a Christian, also Easy Spelling, Golden Alphabet, A New Alphabet on the Bible and the Church Catechism, Illustrated Testament and Spiritual Railway, Bible Alphabet, Zion's Bank, Death and the Lady, Prodigal Daughter, The Prince of Wales Pocket Primer,** with several alphabets, etc., all measuring between circa $2\frac{1}{4}$ by $1\frac{7}{8}$, $1\frac{3}{4}$ by $1\frac{3}{4}$ or $1\frac{5}{8}$ by $1\frac{1}{2}$ inches. It would be almost impossible to come across such a large collection of characteristic ephemera anywhere else.

The concern with miniature books nurtured at the Bodleian Library, the official library of Oxford University, is evidenced even in their publicity. I believe they are alone in this country to publish a special postcard illustrating some of their possessions in that field. They are giving it thus the stamp of approval of one of the most venerable institutions in the world. The card I have before me

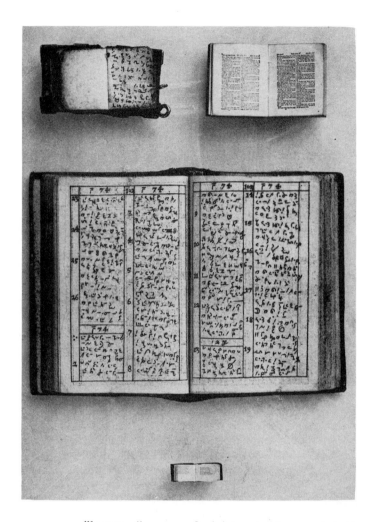

illustrates "a group of miniature books, actual size". They are Jeremiah Rich's **Psalms** in shorthand, printed circa 1670, **The Rose Garden of Omar Khayyam,** printed in Worcester, Mass. in 1932 and a unique tiny manuscript sermon in shorthand by Rich, circa 1650. Amongst other rare miniature items, the Bodleian owns the unique copy of the first edition of John Taylor's **The booke of martyrs,** 1616.

The Mitchell Library, part of the Glasgow Public Libraries, has a comprehensive collection of the miniature books published by David Bryce and Son of that city.

In the United States there exist many collections of miniature books in public institutions. The best-known one is that of the Grolier Club in the City of New York, a venerable and highly-esteemed body of bibliophiles founded in 1884. The club published a concise list of their holdings of "microscopic books" in 1911 when they comprised 176 items. Since then the collection has grown to at least twice that size and we have seen a supplementary typewritten list which adds many coveted titles to those enumerated in the printed volume. The Grolier Club miniatures include many splendid tiny almanacs from various countries, the diminutive Meigs **Rubaiyat,** many thumb Bibles, fine volumes printed by Didot, Jannon, Barbou, Pickering, Salmin and others, not all of them under three inches high but in their majority of very small format indeed.

We have already referred to the Library of Congress in Washington which has a considerable collection of miniature volumes including some incunabula although the latter are larger than 3 inches. The library clearly demonstrated their great interest in that field when they exhibited part of the Stanley Marcus collection.

The Public Library of Worcester, Massachusetts started a "Dolls' Library" in 1927. The New York Public Library organised an important exhibition jointly sponsored by the "LXIVmos" from 26th December 1928 to the 1st of April 1929 which contained 60 miniature Bibles, circa 60 classical texts in various languages while a special case was reserved for English classics such as Shakespeare, Burns, Bunyan, Tennyson and Dickens. 19 miniature newspapers were also included.

The International Year of the Child was celebrated by the Chicago Public Library with an exhibition in November and December 1979, featuring selections from the libraries of Stanley

Marcus and Foreman M. Lebold under the title "The Curious World of Miniature Books". The latter collection of 165 volumes had been donated by that lady and included books from the seventeenth century to date collected over a period of 30 years. The illustrated leaflet issued to advertise the exhibition contained a special "introduction for young readers" in addition to a history of miniature books.

Monsignor Francis J. Weber mentions in his **Minibibliophilia** to which we have already referred in this chapter, that the Huntington Library in San Marino, California, possess 467 miniature volumes while smaller Californian collections exist at the William Andrews Clark Library, Los Angeles and the University of California Library at Santa Barbara.

We must assume that the lively production of miniature books in present day America has encouraged many other public libraries to start special collections.

In a chapter dealing with collectors and collections, brief reference should be made to the special miniature bookplates so many bibliophiles have had

MINIATURE HISTORY OF ENGLAND, London, Goode Bros. Frontispiece and title page

designed for their treasures. To mention just a few we have ourselves seen, we know of those of Dr. Spielmann, Dr. Samuel Hordes, a collector of Hebrew miniatures, Ruth Adomeit, Julian Edison, Stanley Marcus, Arthur Houghton, Jr., Wilbur Macey Stone, Robert Massmann, Masatoki Hanzawa, Rene Mamelsdorf (*ex libris minimis*), Francis J. Weber (*Ex Minilibris*), Charles Elton, Maurice Baring and Pierre Lévy Haas, whose curious bookplate shows the face of a donkey with the motto *Je m'obstine* (I persevere obstinately). Ernest H. Shephard, the famous illustrator, designed a special tiny bookplate for the volumes in Queen Mary's Dolls' House measuring $2\frac{1}{32}$ by $\frac{1}{2}$ inches bearing the Queen's monogram "M.R."

A. Horodisch of Amsterdam, himself a miniature book collector of long standing, published in 1966 a volume **Miniatur Exlibris** in 200 numbered copies with 14 full-page plates and 15 illustrations in the text which he issued from his own firm Erasmus in Amsterdam, size $2\frac{1}{4}$ by $2\frac{1}{8}$ inches, with German text and a summary in English.

Miniature books in original cases.

CONCLUSION

The preceding chapters have attempted to take the reader on a guided tour through the world of miniature books. We trust that it will have conveyed an idea of the incomparable richness, variety and fascination of this specialised field of book-collecting. Many of the pinnacles of world literature are available in such a small physical size, in no way diminished in their impact on the mind but brought closer to the reader than ever before, making them constant companions rather than exhibits ranged on the shelves of public or private libraries. Their very portability marries them more intimately to their owners and permits easy and frequent reference to their contents whenever desired.

The same considerations apply to many of the special subjects treated in miniature books, to the rich harvest of tiny children's books and, of course, to various reference works like encyclopedias, dictionaries, technical tables, statistics and pictorial documentation.

Above all, these minute tomes are, for those of us who have learned to love and cherish them, tangible manifestations of the infinite variety of human skills, sharpened and refined by the exigencies of their format.

It cannot be doubted that miniature books sprung from a deep-seated desire in many people, maybe an almost primeval longing of man for small things, for portability, accessibility and even more, for perfection. Proof of this can be seen in the fact that such minute volumes have been a feature of book production even before the advent of printing, and have remained a persistent phenomenon throughout the ensuing centuries right up to the present day.

Knowledge is an important aid to conservation. May we therefore express the hope that this book, by signposting the significant highlights as well as some narrow bypaths of miniature book making, will help to gain new friends for this many-sided hobby and make those already addicted to it more aware of the achievements of the past. If that is so, we will have made a worthwhile contribution to one of the most satisfying and exciting facets of bookcollecting.

BIBLIOGRAPHY

Adomeit (Ruth E.; Editor) The Miniature Book Collector. Published quarterly. Vol. I, Nos. 1-4; Vol. II, Nos. 1-4, June 1960 to March 1962. Worcester, Mass., Achille J. St. Onge. Index volume of 40 pages edited by Robert E. Massmann issued by The Lilliputter Press, Woodstock, Vermont, in 1963.
Adomeit, (Ruth E.) Three Centuries of Thumb Bibles. A Checklist, 430 pp., many illustrations. New York, Garland Publishing Inc., 1980. Lists ca. 280 items dating from 1601 to 1890.
American Art Association. Sale Catalogue "An unusual collection of miniature books, formed by a lady", 18 illustrations, 700 copies printed. Comprises 204 items. New York, 1928.
Andrews (William Loring) Sexto-Decimos et Infra XXIV, 118pp., 25 illustrs. New York, Charles Scribner, 1899.
Bain (Iain) Albert Schloss's Bijou Almanacs 1839-1843. Reprinted from the original steel plates, with an introduction by Iain Bain. 19 pp. of text with illustrations. 150 numbered copies printed. London, Nattali & Maurice, 1969.
Blackwell (B. H., Ltd) Catalogue No. 774 "Microbiblia. A Collection of Small Books". Lists 329 items, not all below the 3-inch limit. Oxford 1963.
Blumenthal (Walter Hart) Formats and Foibles. A few books which might be called curious. 2 ff., 105 pp. Includes reference to miniature books and is itself one, measuring $2\frac{7}{16}$ by 2 inches. Worcester, Mass., Achille St. Onge, 1956.

Bondy (Louis W.) 4-page article "Miniature Books" in "Books. The Journal of the National Book League", issue No. 353. London, May-June, 1964.
Bondy (Louis W.) 7-page article "Miniature Books. Their History and Significance" in "Antiquarian Book Monthly Review", Volume VII, No. 1. With 6 illustrations. Oxford, January, 1980.
Book Auction Records. These annual volumes provided a separate heading for miniature books sold singly (not in lots) until that admirable feature was abandoned with volume 72 for the years 1974-1975. London & later Farnham, Henry Stevens, Sons & Stiles, and from volume 65 onwards Folkestone and London, Dawsons of Pall Mall.
Brunet (Jacques-Charles) Manuel du Libraire. 6 volumes and 2 supplements. Contains numerous references to miniature books under their authors. Paris, Firmin Didot Frères, 1860-1878.
Buza (Márton) Magyar miniatür könyvek bibliográfiája 1692-1973 (bibliography of Hungarian miniature books). 118 pp. listing 476 items. Budapest, Miniatürkönyv-Gyüjtök Klubja (miniature booklovers club), 1974.
Castaing (Roger) Almanachs minuscules français. (extrait du no. 1, 1959 du Bulletin du Bibliophile). 15pp., 2 full-page plates of illustrations. Paris, L. Giraud-Badin, 1959.
Čubar'jan (Ogán Stepanocič) 9-page article "Sowjetische Miniaturbücher" including a list of miniature books published in the German Democratic

Republic, in "Marginalien. Zeitschrift für Buchkunst und Bibliophilie", No. 52. Berlin-Erkner, 1973.

De Vinne (Theodore) "Brilliants, a setting of humorous poetry in Brilliant types". The preface to this tiny volume by the famous American printer contains a history of miniature printing. $2\frac{1}{4}$ by $1\frac{9}{16}$ inches. New York, The De Vinne Press, 1895.

DuCann (C. G. L.) 3-page illustrated article "These little books are bound to amuse" in "Art & Antiques Weekly", Vol. 7, No. 4. London, August 19, 1972.

Edison (Julian I.: Editor) Miniature Book News. Periodical from No. 1 to 44 (to date). Many illustrations. St. Louis, Missouri, September 1965 to March 1981.

Elton (C. & M.) Little Books. 10 leaves. 2 pages of illustrations. Reprint of 15-page article in "Bibliographica", part 10, published in London in 1896, Lake Worth, Florida, Ford Press, 1977.

Feffer (Solomon) 7-page article "Hebrew Miniature Books" on pages 384 to 390 of the book "Essays on Jewish Booklore" edited by Philip Goodman, New York, Ktav Publishing House, Jewish Book Council of America, 1971.

Grand-Carteret (John) Les Almanachs Français. Bibliographie, Iconographie (1600-1895). CX, 846, 1 pp., numerous illustrations. 1250 numbered copies. Lists many French miniature almanacs. Paris, J. Alisie et Cie., 1896.

Graves (Robert) "Poems: Abridged for Dolls and Princes". A facsimile reproduction of the miniature volume hand-written by the author for Queen Mary's Dolls' House, enlarged from the original. London, Cassell & Company Ltd., 1971.

Grolier Club (The) of the City of New York. A Short List of Microscopic Books in the Library of the Grolier Club, mostly presented by Samuel P. Avery (this is an extract of the Annual Report). 15-page introduction on the history of miniature books and lists 176 items. New York, 1911.

Gumuchian & Cie. Les Livres de l'Enfance du XVe au XIXe Siècle. Catalogue XIII, 2 volumes, the second with illustrations only. Has section of Miniature Books from item 4048 to item 4140. One of 1000 copies. Paris, no date.

Hanson (Robert F.: Editor) The Microbibliophile. A bi-monthly review of the literature concerning miniature books. Volume I, No. 1 was published in March 1977. Mattituck, N.Y., Robert F. Hanson.

Henderson (James D.; Editor) The Newsletter of the LXIVmos. Complete in 21 issues. Re-issued in book form with a foreword and index by Robert E. Massmann, originally published between November 1927 and November 1929. Woodstock, Vermont, The Lilliputter Press, 1968.

Henderson (James D.) Lilliputian Newspapers. Foreword by R. W. G. Vail. 95 pp., illustrations and samples of actual newspapers. Printed in 1000 copies. Worcester, Mass., Achille J. St. Onge, 1936.

Hillside Press (The), Bibliography of. Preface by Robert E. Massmann. XIX, 51 pp. Size $2\frac{5}{16}$ by $1\frac{15}{16}$ inches. Tilton, New Hampshire, 1971.

Hodgson (J. E.) Six-page article "Miniature Books for Collectors", illustrated, in "The Connoisseur". London, August, 1936.

Horodisch (Abraham) $11\frac{1}{2}$-page illustrated article "Über Bücher kleinsten Formats" (about books of the smallest size) in "Börsenblatt für den Deutschen Buchhandel", Frankfurt edition, No. 17, February 28, 1978.

Horodisch (Abraham) 25-page article "Het kleine Boek in Nederland" (the small book in the Netherlands) in 2 parts, published in "Biblion", Organ of the Dutch Antiquarian Booktrade, Nos. 2 and 3. Amsterdam, 25th September 1940 and 15th February 1941.

Horodisch (Abraham) Miniatur Exlibris. German text with English summary. 95 pp., 15 illustrations, some in colour, plus 14 pages of bookplates printed from the original blocks. 200

numbered copies printed. Amsterdam, Erasmus, 1966. Size $2\frac{7}{16}$ by $2\frac{1}{4}$ inches.

Houghton Jr. (Arthur A.) Sale catalogue "The Collection of Miniature Books formed by Arthur A. Houghton, Jr." 96, 4 pp., 22 plates, incl. 3 in colour, listing 351 lots. London, Christie, Manson & Wood, Ltd., 5th December, 1979.

Houghton Jr. (Arthur A.) Sale catalogue "Books and Manuscripts from the Library of Arthur A. Houghton, Jnr. Part II: M-Z". Lists under Nos. 341, 362, 527 and 528 four miniature volumes of exceptional importance, with illustrations (by Martin Parker, George Peel and John Weever). London, Christie, Manson & Wood Ltd., 11th and 12th June, 1980.

Janka (Gyula) Bibliography of Miniature Books (Hungarian ones only) 1945-70; 1971-1972; 1973-1974; 1975. Together 4 volumes. English, Hungarian and Russian text. 235, 233, 325, 237 pp., listing and illustrating 462 volumes. Budapest, Müszaki Könyvkiadó, 1972-77. Size of the volumes $2\frac{13}{16}$ by $2\frac{1}{16}$ inches.

Janka (Gyula) Miniatür Könyvek Története és Gyüjtése (history and collecting of miniature books). Text in Hungarian. 81 pp., illustrations. Printed in 250 numbered copies. Budapest, Egyetemi Nyomda Kollektivaia (collective of the University Press), 1969. Size $2\frac{5}{16}$ by $1\frac{5}{8}$ inches.

Janka (Gyula) Advises (!) for Collectors of Miniature Books. English and Hungarian text. 151 pp., illustrations. 500 copies printed. Budapest, Egyetemi Nyomda, 1971. Size $2\frac{5}{16}$ by $1\frac{5}{8}$ inches.

Janka (Gyula) The International Miniature Book Collection. English, Hungarian and German text. 203 pp., illustrations. 4100 copies printed of which 1000 are numbered. Budapest, Egyetemi Nyomda, 1972. Size $2\frac{5}{16}$ by $1\frac{5}{8}$ inches.

Janka (Gyula) About Miniature Books for Collectors. English, Hungarian, German and Russian text. 251 pp., illustrations. Budapest, Muszaki Nyomda, 1973.

Size $2\frac{5}{16}$ by $1\frac{5}{8}$ inches. 4000 copies printed.

Janka (Gyula) What we should know about Miniature Books. English, Hungarian, German and Russian text. 268 pp., illustrations. Budapest, Egyetemi Nyomda, 1974. Size $2\frac{5}{16}$ by $1\frac{5}{8}$ inches.

Janka (Gyula) Editor Mikrobibliofilok. Illustrated periodical in Hungarian language. Organ of the Miniature Booklovers Club. Budapest, Egyetemi Nyomda, from January 1971.

Janka (Gyula) 2-page illustrated article "Miniature Books" in "Print in Britain", London, Vol. 11, No. 8, December 1963.

Johnson (Col. William) A Bibliography of the Thumb Bibles of John Taylor. 13 pp., 2 leaves of illustrations. Printed in 40 copies for private distribution. Aberdeen, printed at the University Press, 1910.

Kardos (Gyula) The Nestor of collectors of Miniature Books. Published on the occasion of the 60th birthday of Gyula Janka. English, Hungarian and Russian text. 289 pp., illustrations. Printed in 450 copies. Budapest, Egyetemi Nyomda, 1974. Size $2\frac{9}{16}$ by $1\frac{3}{4}$ inches.

Kleemeier (Fr. J.) 10-page article "Kleine Bücher und mikroskopische Drucke" (small books and microscopic printing) in Börsenblatt für den deutschen Buchhandel, 73rd year, Nos. 131 and 132. Lists many miniature books with their precise measurements. Leipzig, 9th and 11th June, 1906.

Kuczynski (Arnold) Verzeichnis einer Sammlung mikroskopicher Drucke und Formate im Besitze von Albert Brockhaus in Leipzig (list of a collection of microscopic printings and formats in the possession of Albert Brockhaus). 42 pp., lists 98 items. Leipzig, F. A. Brockhaus, 1888.

Leningrad. Catalogue of the Exhibition of Miniature Editions at the Leningrad Society of Bibliophiles. Text in Russian. 40 pp., 1 plate of illustrations. Leningrad, 1927.

Lucas (E. V.) The Book of the Queen's Dolls' House Library. XIV, 384 pp., 24 plates of which 8 are in colour. 1500 numbered copies printed. London, Methuen & Co., 1924.

Lüthi (Karl J.) Bücher kleinsten Formats (books of the smallest size). 40 pp., 8 plates, 8 text illustrs. Text of a lecture given to the Swiss Society of Bibliophiles which describes the Vera von Rosenberg collection of miniature books. Bern, Buchdruckerei Büchler & Co., 1924.

McCormick, (Edith) 5-page illustrated article "Minding the Miniatures" in "American Libraries", published by the American Library Association, March 1980. Chiefly based on Stanley Marcus' collection and publishing.

MacFarlane (Harold) 6-page article "A Library within a Library" in "Pall Mall Magazine". 9 illustrations. Deals with small books in the British Museum Library. London, October, 1902.

Manners (Guy) One-page article "Tom Thumb's Library" in "Investor's Chronicle". London, 6th June, 1969.

Marcus (Stanley) & Stone (Marvin) "Why Miniature Books". 16 pp. 500 numbered copies printed. Published on the occasion of an exhibition of miniature books from the Collection of Mr. and Mrs. Stanley Marcus. Dallas, Texas, Friends of the Dallas Public Library, 1976.

Mikrobibliofilok. See Janka.

Mikrobiblion. Das Buch von den kleinen Büchern (the book of the small books). Introductory chapter by Kurt Freyer. Bibliography of the Vera von Rosenberg collection by Robert W. Petri, 176 pp., listing 254 items. 426 numbered copies. Berlin, Horodisch & Marx Verlag, 1929.

Miniature Book Collector. See Adomeit.

Miniature Book News. See Edison.

Mohr (Louis) Des Impressique Microscopiques. 11 pp., 100 copies printed. Paris, Edouard Rouveyre, 1879.

Nauroy (Ch.) Bibliographie des Impressions Microscopiques. 127 pp., 250 numbered copies. Paris, Charavay, 1881.

Newsletter of the LXIVmos. See Henderson.

Pollard (A. F. C.) "Miniature and Microscopic Documents". Presidential address 1943, reprinted in "The Proceedings of the British Society for International Bibliography", Vol. V, Part 3, pages 43 to 54. London, 28th September, 1943.

Prager (R. L.) 8-page chapter "Kleine Bücher und mikroskopische Drucke" in "Jahrbuch Deutscher Bibliophilen und Literaturfreunde", pages 93 to 100. Vienna, 1917.

Roscoe (Sidney) Illustrated 9-page article "John Marshall and 'The Infant's Library'," in "The Book Collector", Vol. 4, No. 2, London, Summer 1955.

Schäfer Wolf (Else) Lilliputiana. In the Danish language. 22 pp., limited edition for the members of the Dansk Bibliofil-Klub. Copenhagen, Det Berlingske Bogtrykkeri, 1951.

Sheringham (H. T.) A Library in Miniature. 79 pages, 4 illustrations. 500 copies printed. London, The Java Head, 1948. Reprints an article published in "The Connoisseur", London in August and November, 1902, with 16 illustrations.

Spielmann (Percy Edwin) Catalogue of the Library of Miniature Books collected by Percy Edwin Spielmann ... together with some Descriptive Summaries. XV, 289 pp., 4 plates, listing 541 items. 500 numbered copies. London, Edward Arnold, 1961.

Spielmann (P. E.) Sale catalogue "of Printed Books comprising ... the well-known Collection of Miniature Books formed by the late Dr. Percy Edwin Spielmann."Item No. 439 lists a considerable number of the 848 volumes in the collection. London, Sotheby's, 20th and 21st July, 1964.

Sternaux (Ludwig) Illustrated $3\frac{1}{2}$-page article "Bücher kleinsten Formats" (books of the smallest size) in "Philobiblion", eine Zeitschrift für Bücherfreunde, No. 2. Vienna, Herbert Reichner, May, 1928.

Stone (Wilbur Macey) A Snuff-Boxful of Bibles. 110 pp., illustrated. 200 copies printed. Newark, Carteret Book Club, 1926.

Stone (Wilbur Macey) The Thumb Bible of John Taylor. 72 pp., 9 illustrations. 100 copies printed. Brookline, Mass., The LXIVmos, March 1928.

Stone (Wilbur Macey) The Gigantick Histories of Thomas Boreman. 41 pp., illustrated. 250 copies printed. Describes the famous 18th century English children's books. Portland, Maine, The Southworth Press, 1933.

Thompson (Eben Francis) A Thimbleful of Books, being some account of small books in all ages and more particularly of The Smallest Printed Book in the World. 36 pp., illustrated. Privately Printed. Worcester, Massachusetts, 1933.

Times Literary Supplement. "Miniature Books". A general survey in the issue. London, 20th September, 1923.

Tissandier (Gaston) Livres Minuscules. La plus grande bibliothèque des plus petits livres du monde. Collection de M. Georges Solomon. 20 pp., 7 text illustrations. Paris, G. Masson, 1894.

Tuneewa (Mrs. A.) 21-page article "Miniature Books in the State Library at Odessa" in "Zentralblatt für Bibliothekswesen", Leipzig, November 1926.

Weber (Megr. Francis J.) Minibibliophilia. 30 pages. 250 copies printed. Los Angeles, Dawson's, 1979. Size $2\frac{3}{4}$ by $2\frac{1}{8}$ inches.

Some booksellers' and auctioneers' catalogues also provide much information on miniature books. They are a regular feature in the catalogues of Dawson's Book Shop, Los Angeles; K. Gregory, New York; Bromer, Watertown, Mass.; H. M. Fletcher, London; Louis W. Bondy, London; Sotheby Parke Bernet & Co., especially the auction sales of Children's Books and Juvenilia at their auction rooms in London; The Swann Galleries, Inc., New York.

GENERAL INDEX

(followed by an index of publishers and printers)
The page numbers of illustrations are given in bold type

209

213

214

INDEX OF PUBLISHERS AND PRINTERS

219